Building Stronger Marriages and Families

Making Your House a Home

Building Stronger Marriages and Families

Making Your House a Home

by
Billy Joe Daugherty

Harrison House
Tulsa, Oklahoma

6th Printing

Building Stronger Marriages and Families —
Making Your House a Home
ISBN 0-89274-858-3
Copyright © 1991 by Billy Joe Daugherty
Victory Christian Center
7700 South Lewis Avenue
Tulsa, Oklahoma 74136-7700

Published by Harrison House, Inc.
P. O. Box 35035
Tulsa, Oklahoma 74153

Contents

Introduction

Successful Christian marriages are made up of successful Christian individuals who get together. When you put two people together who are walking in harmony with God, they'll walk in harmony with each other. If you are living in harmony with God, you can live in harmony with those in your family, whether it's your husband or wife, your children, or your parents.

However, just being a Christian doesn't guarantee good marriage and family relationships. In Hosea 4:6 the Lord says, **"My people are destroyed for lack of knowledge...."**

Sharon and I have a good marriage. It's getting better every year. We have four children who love God. We're under construction, and God's not finished with us yet! We've stayed together. We still love each other. So while we haven't been married as long as others, we believe we do have some things to impart to strengthen your marriage and family relationships.

We're fighting one of the greatest battles in America in this hour, and that is the battle for the marriage and the home. The little things that we're talking about may seem insignificant to you, but Satan has taken them, as small as they are, and has driven a wedge between marriage partners and their children. If we'll root them out and make an effort to do the things that God has spoken for us to do in His Word, we'll see marriages last. We're praying for marriages and homes to be strong.

Perhaps you've been married before and you've remarried. We're not condemning you for past mistakes.

We want the marriage you're in to last and be strong. If you've gone through a broken marriage, perhaps you'll be remarried. We want that marriage to last. It's possible that you'll be restored to your original mate. We've had the wonderful privilege of remarrying a number of people in our congregation.

In this book, you'll find several scriptural principles that will give you a basis for better marriage and family relationships.

Although the enemy is interested in destroying marriages and families because this is the basis of what makes up the Church, he cannot do so if you'll chart the course of your marriage and family relationships on the Word of God. Today is the best day to begin!

— Billy Joe Daugherty

1
Marriage —
God's First Institution

Marriage was the first institution created by God. Whenever you start talking about the marriage, home, and family, God gets involved.

God said of the marriage institution, **Therefore a man shall leave his father and mother and be joined to his wife, and they shall become** *one flesh* (Gen. 2:24).

The joining together of the husband and wife is the smallest cell of the Church: two people who love God coming together as one.

Not everyone is called to marriage, however. I believe God has called some people to a life of singleness. God has called me to be married, and in the marriage, He hasn't taken away from my effectiveness in ministry, but by giving me a mate who's turned on to God, He has multiplied my effectiveness in ministry.

There can be a blessing either way. Just because you're married doesn't mean you can't be effective in the work of the ministry.

2
Prime Rib: A "Help Meet"

In Genesis 1, God created man and the animals, but there was no suitable companion or "help meet" for Adam. There was no one with whom he could fellowship.

In Genesis 2:18, God said, ... "It is not good that man should be alone; I will make him a *helper* comparable to him." The *King James Version* says, ... I will make him an *help meet* for him. The word *meet* means "suited, qualified, adapted, complementary, or compatible." In other words the Lord said, "Let's make a helper suitable for Adam (or for man)."

> Out of the ground the Lord God formed every beast of the field and every bird of the air, and brought them to Adam to see what he would call them. And whatever Adam called each living creature, that was its name.
>
> So Adam gave names to all cattle, to the birds of the air, and to every beast of the field. But for Adam there was not found a helper comparable to him.
>
> And the Lord God caused a deep sleep to fall on Adam, and he slept; and He took one of his ribs, and closed up the flesh in its place.
>
> Then the rib which the Lord God had taken from man He made into a woman, and He brought her to the man.
>
> And Adam said: "This is now bone of my bones and flesh of my flesh; she shall be called Woman, because she was taken out of Man."
>
> **Genesis 2:19-23**

God took a rib out of Adam, and He made Prime Rib! You may be questioning, "How did God make woman out of a rib?" I don't know. He just did. There's a lot of things I don't know, like, "Why does a kangaroo have a pouch? Or why does a giraffe have a long neck?"

God can do anything He wants to do. Jesus caused maimed limbs to be restored, so certainly God could take a rib or a side of man and fashion a woman out of it. If He could take the dust from the earth and make a man, then He could make a woman from a rib!

God made the woman to be with the man as a companion. Adam was lonely. He had everything in the world he could possibly need, but there was a loneliness (an emptiness) on the inside of him that wasn't satisfied. Eve filled this need. She completed Adam, just as God has created wives today to complete their husbands.

3

Leaving and Cleaving

Therefore a man shall leave his father and mother and be joined to his wife, and they shall become one flesh.

Genesis 2:24

One of the most important things about really loving your mate in a covenant relationship is leaving your family. Some people never get around to leaving. The apron strings are still tied, and Mama is still helping her little child make decisions. When you leave home to get married, it's time to cut the apron strings.

This goes for women as well as men: leave Mama's influence and control over your life when you join yourself to your mate. The Bible says there's a leaving and then there's a cleaving. This means, as husband and wife, you're drawn together *apart* from the relationship from whence you've come!

There's a sign in the window of a jewelry shop in Los Angeles that typifies the attitude of society in some circles today. It's contrary to what I'm sharing with you. The sign says, "Wedding rings for rent." This is not for people who intend to cleave to their mates. They simply view marriage like this: "If it doesn't work out, then I'll just say good-bye and that'll be it."

A husband and wife are to cleave to each other. *If you'll cleave, it won't be as easy to leave!*

...and they shall become one flesh (Gen. 2:24). In marriage, God has called two to become one, to be united in attitude, mind, vision, and direction. This is why singles need to come to a unity of mind and heart before they marry. Many people simply come to a unity in an attitude of the physical relationship, but they never come to a unity in their mind, vision, direction, intention, and purpose in life.

Many people marry and later discover that the person they married has a different plan for life. They say, "I didn't know that's what he (or she) wanted to do." Yet, I'm wondering, "How did they ever get married without coming to that place of unity?" It takes time to understand what another person plans to do with his or her life. It usually doesn't come in three weeks or even in three months.

When a pilot makes plans to land on the runway of an airport, he aligns himself with the runway a long time before he touches down. He checks on a perfect directional that will touch the plane down on a strategic spot where he can stop the aircraft so it won't go off the end of the runway.

How much more important it is in our lives that we align ourselves and get on target before we touch down in a marriage relationship — that we align ourselves in unity one with another.

If you can't come to a place of unity in the dating relationship, then you should say, "Let's postpone the wedding." The postponement is much better than the divorce of a relationship. Take a few more months. Many marriages would have been saved if the bride and groom had waited until they came to a unity and worked things out before the wedding.

4

Intimacy
in the Marriage Relationship

**And they were both naked, the man and his wife,
and were not ashamed.**

Genesis 2:25

God intends that there be an intimacy between the
husband and wife so the physical, emotional, and total
needs of both can be met in that relationship. This kind of
intimacy takes work. It takes commitment. It takes the grace
of God to bring two people into a place where they each
leave, cleave, and come into unity and intimacy as husband
and wife.

Intimacy is the willingness to be open and transparent
with your mate. It is the sharing of thoughts, dreams,
desires, and feelings in a free and flowing relationship.
Nothing is hidden or restrained in a truly intimate
relationship. There is no shame, fear, or embarrassment in
this level of love.

To develop intimacy at all levels in every phase of a
relationship takes time. Don't be discouraged if it doesn't
happen immediately. On the other side, continue to believe
for God's best.

5

God's Plan for Marriage

God's plan for man was that He indwell the marriage, the home, and the family.

> Then God said, "Let Us make man in Our image, according to Our likeness; *let them have dominion* over the fish of the sea, over the birds of the air, and over the cattle, over all the earth and over every creeping thing that creeps on the earth."
>
> So God created man in His own image; in the image of God He created him; male and female He created them.
>
> Then God blessed them, and God said to them, "*Be fruitful and multiply;* fill the earth and subdue it; *have dominion* over the fish of the sea, over the birds of the air, and over every living thing that moves on the earth."
>
> **Genesis 1:26-28**

It is God's plan for the husband and wife to come together in agreement and *take dominion and authority to stop the works of the devil and bring the earth under subjection to God's plan.*

There's no stronger power of agreement on earth than in the marriage union, because in Christ, the husband and wife are one. Jesus said, "...where two or three are gathered together in My name, I am there in the midst of them" (Matt. 18:20).

God suggests the impact of "two in agreement" in preference to one in Deuteronomy 32:30. He says that one can put a thousand to flight, but *two can put ten thousand to flight!*

It's a shocking statistic that in this hour, more than 50 percent of the new marriages in our country are ending in divorce. This statistic appears to be about as accurate in Christian circles as in ungodly circles. I'm convinced that we can change this statistic if we'll study God's Word to gain an understanding of His principles for dating, marriage, the home and family and then obey His Word.

One of the most distressing things we're seeing in this hour is people who have been married 25 to 30 years (or more) suddenly calling it quits saying, "I don't want to live together with that person anymore."

These statistics, obviously, affect the godly seed that is produced in the marriage union.

God created the man and woman to be together to literally fill the earth with godly children. He made the man and the woman in such a way so they could reproduce after their own kind. In Genesis 1:28, God said to Adam and Eve, ..."**Be fruitful and multiply; fill the earth and subdue it....**"

The godly seed, as we'll discuss in more depth later, is to play a major role today in taking dominion over the enemy and bringing the earth into subjection to God's plan.

6

The Sacredness of Marriage

There's a sacredness about marriage. It's called "holy matrimony" because God is to be the Third Party witness to the marriage union.

I'm sure you have attended marriage ceremonies in which the minister talked about the man and wife being "joined" together. Two people can become one flesh physically, *but only God can put them together spiritually.*

In the Old Testament, marriage was so holy that when a man and woman came together as husband and wife, if it was discovered that the wife had been unfaithful before marriage, she was publicly stoned to death by the people. Thank God we live in a day of grace!

In the Old Testament, God placed a sacredness over the marriage union, because He wanted it to be holy, honorable, and blessed. God hasn't changed. Marriage is still to be holy, honorable, and blessed.

7

Scriptural Covenant Agreements

The marriage covenant was the first institution established by God. From the very beginning, God put a man and a woman together. In marriage, the man and woman become a part of each other. They are united as one.

In Hebrew the word translated *covenant* means "to cut, to make an incision where blood flows."

Several covenants are mentioned in Scripture. We'll examine a few of them.

1. *God made a covenant with Abram,* promising to bless him and to make him into a great nation. (Gen. 17:2-9.)

2. *God made a covenant with Noah* when He put a rainbow in the sky and said He would not destroy the earth again with a flood. When Noah stepped out of the ark, he offered a sacrifice, which symbolized that he was in covenant relationship with God. (Gen. 9:8-17.)

3. *There was a covenant of friendship between Jonathan and David.* We might call it a blood-brother covenant. (1 Sam. 18:1-4.)

4. *A covenant was established between God and the children of Israel on the night of the Passover.* God told the Israelites that He would be their God and the Provider of everything they needed. He revealed Himself as a covenant-keeping God. (Ex. 12:1-13.)

5. *Jesus brought us into a New Covenant.* **"For this is My blood of the new covenant, which is shed for many for the remission of sins"** (Matt. 26:28).

God does things in the earth through human beings. Even the sending of His Son, Jesus Christ, came through the faith of Abraham and the faith of a teenage girl by the name of Mary who believed God.

The New Covenant is similar to the type of covenant established with the Israelites on the night of the Passover. The covenant was set before them. They ate of the body of the lamb that had been roasted. The blood was sprinkled on the door posts, so they would be delivered from the angel of death. That night they were delivered as a covenant people.

In the New Covenant spoken of in Matthew 26:28, Jesus was willing, first of all, to give His life for us. The most precious and priceless thing that God had was His Son, but because God is a covenant-keeping God, He was willing to give His Son to save us from our sin.

When we put our faith in Jesus Christ, we enter into this covenant. Then, in turn, we commit our entire lives unto God, for we are not our own. Everything that we have, if God calls for it, we give. That's why to be saved, we must confess the lordship of Jesus Christ: Jesus is Lord, He is ruler, He is the King of our lives.

Some people receive forgiveness only so they'll miss hell, but God is calling us into a covenant relationship so we will commit everything that is ours unto Him to be used for His purposes.

8

God — Third Party to the Marriage Covenant

The most important thing for you to realize is that marriage is a covenant relationship to which God is a party. Marriage is not something you can cast away any time you want. I say that you cannot, in the name of Jesus. I come against that kind of thinking. In marriage, you are in covenant agreement, and God doesn't see you and your mate as two. He sees you as *one*.

It may be that one partner is weaker than the other. If you are the stronger one, you may have to bear the burdens of the weaker. But if you'll stand in agreement with God, He'll move in behalf of your marriage, and bring you into harmony together.

> **Wives, submit to your own husbands, as to the Lord.**
>
> **For the husband is head of the wife, as also Christ is the head of the church; and He is the Savior of the body.**
>
> **Therefore, just as the church is subject to Christ, so let the wives be to their own husbands in everything.**
>
> **Husbands, love your wives, just as Christ also loved the church and gave Himself for it.**
>
> **Ephesians 5:22-25**

From this text, we always want to shout, "Wives, submit." But in the covenant relationship, the husband must be committed to give his life for his wife. God is saying

22

to the husband, "I'm calling you to give your whole life for your wife, to give everything that you are in behalf of your covenant relationship of marriage." Now, this is why the Lord gave His life:

> **that He might sanctify and cleanse it with the washing of water by the word,**
>
> **that He might present it to Himself a glorious church, not having spot or wrinkle or any such thing, but that it should be holy and without blemish.**
>
> **Ephesians 5:26,27**

The purpose of Jesus' giving His life was so a holy, pure bride might be prepared. Then Paul says:

> **So husbands ought to love their own wives *as their own bodies;* he who loves his wife loves himself.**
>
> **For no one ever hated his own flesh, but nourishes and cherishes it, just as the Lord does the church.**
>
> **Ephesians 5:28,29**

When your flesh wants to eat, you feed it. When your flesh wants to sleep, you sleep. When your flesh wants to sit down, you rest it for a while. You take care of the flesh. If the flesh gets hurt, you doctor it. Without flesh, you wouldn't be you!

Now, I'm not talking about carnality as flesh, but I'm talking about the flesh and bone that's around your spirit being. There's nothing wrong with the physical body in which you live. In fact, it can be alive with the life of Jesus Christ. It can actually be infused with God's life. The mortal body can carry you somewhere to preach the Gospel. The flesh can go somewhere and tell someone how to get healed and saved.

The body is going to be resurrected and glorified one day, so we're to take care of it. Jesus is saying, "Take care of your wife in the same way you do your own flesh." When you start thinking about your mate, start thinking about how you would take care of yourself.

For we are members of His body, of His flesh and of His bones.

"For this reason a man shall leave his father and mother and be joined to his wife, and the two shall become one flesh."

Ephesians 5:30,31

Just as you are united with Christ, so you are united with your mate. A husband and wife are linked together as one in a covenant relationship. God sees you and your mate as one.

You maintain your separate identity in the same way that the Father, Son, and Holy Spirit are three separate identifiable persons, yet representing separate ministries. They make up the Trinity, the three in one.

This is a great mystery, but I speak concerning Christ and the church.

Ephesians 5:32

Paul says in Colossians 1:27 that the mystery of the Gospel is ...**Christ in you, the hope of glory.** The mystery of the Gospel is that God actually indwells the believer through the person of the Holy Spirit. We have become one spirit with the Lord. (1 Cor. 6:17.) We are united with Him. This is why we're called *Christ*-ians. We're to be little Christs, made in the image and likeness of God.

Nevertheless let each one of you in particular so love his own wife as himself, and let the wife see that she respects her husband.

Ephesians 5:33

When you were born again, God took the resurrection power of the Holy Spirit and joined you to Jesus. You were not just forgiven of your sins and all that was against you, but something more took place. When you were saved, *you came into a supernatural union with Jesus Christ.*

Remember when Saul was struck down on the Damascus Road and Jesus said, ..."**Saul, Saul, why are**

you persecuting *Me?''* (Acts 9:4). Saul was persecuting Christians, but Jesus said, . . . **''I am Jesus,** *whom you are persecuting.* . . *''* (Acts 9:5). Jesus took the persecution of the Christians as a personal offense, because any person who is born again has come into a supernatural union with Him.

Just as the born-again believer and Jesus are one, when two born-again believers come together in marriage, a miracle takes place and the two become one flesh.

9

Terms of Covenant

A covenant contains elements of a bond, an agreement, or a contract, but a covenant is far more than all of these put together. A covenant involves a union, or a uniting together, and a commitment of one's total life to another.

When God entered into covenant with Abraham, He said, "I am *El Shaddai.*" What He was saying was, "To you, Abraham, and to your seed and your descendants, I'll be yours and theirs. I'll be everything. I'll be whatever you need. If it's healing, if it's strength, if it's to be present with you, to be your joy, to be your peace, to be your Shepherd, I'll be all of these things to you."

In a covenant relationship, each person must be willing to share and impart to the other partner. God called for Abraham's most precious, valued treasure, and that was his son, Isaac, the miracle baby, born when Abraham was 100 years old and Sarah was 90. God called Abraham and told him to go up to Mount Moriah and offer Isaac as a burnt sacrifice. (Gen. 22.)

Abraham obeyed because he was a covenant-keeping man. He understood the terms of a covenant agreement. He knew that when you enter into a covenant with someone, and he calls for something in your life, you're under obligation, agreement, and commitment to give whatever is asked of you.

Contracts, agreements, and bonds have become so commonplace in Western culture that it's nearly impossible to grasp the power of what a covenant agreement meant in Old Testament times.

10

The Sealing of a Covenant

I want to share with you some of the things that have been used to seal a covenant throughout history in the Bible and in various cultures. You'll be able to identify many of them in the marriage covenant:

1. Often, *there was an exchange of coats in pledging oneself to another.* In Africa, covenants were often made between a stronger tribe and a weaker one. A weak tribe would go to a stronger tribe and say, "We want to come into covenant with you for protection." When two tribes were at war, they would often enter into a covenant. One day they would be fighting, and the next day they were the best of friends, walking peaceably with each other. There was an exchange of coats to exemplify ownership.

In the marriage covenant, vows are made in which the couple pledge themselves to one another, and by those vows, there's an exchange: "Everything that I am is yours." There is a joint ownership of goods.

2. *There was an exchange of belts or weapons,* which was a pledge of support and strength.

3. *There was an exchange of names* or a name change. Remember when Abram's name was changed to Abraham and Sarai's to Sarah? (Gen. 17:5; 17:15.) In the New Covenant, when we're born again, we're called "Christian." God then becomes our Father. When Sharon Swift became my wife, her name changed to Sharon Daugherty.

4. *Many times there was an exchange of blood.* The Hebrew word translated *covenant* means ''an incision where blood flows.'' Most often, there would be a third party who would cut the wrists of the two leaders who were entering into covenant. Their blood was mingled, and there was a meal together of bread, wine, and of the mingled blood.

In the New Covenant, this would relate to the joining together physically of the husband and wife in the marriage union.

5. *Blessings and curses are a part of keeping a covenant.* In Deuteronomy 28, the blessings that will come upon you for keeping the covenant are given, as well as the curses that will come if you don't keep the covenant. All through the Bible, there are blessings for keeping the covenant and curses if the covenant is not kept.

6. *Often, an everlasting memorial was established.* On the night of the Passover, the everlasting memorial that was set up was the celebration in which the children of Israel ate the unleavened bread and drank from the cup. God said, **And this day shall be unto you for a memorial; . . . ye shall keep it a feast. . . by an ordinance for ever** (Ex. 12:14 KJV).

The memorial of the New Covenant is that we celebrate Holy Communion, which is a continual reminder of the covenant between us and our Lord.

In the marriage ceremony, we encourage couples to take communion together as a symbol of the covenant in which they're entering. Then there's a blessing that is given in Christian marriages, which is pronounced by the priest or the minister.

The most important thing that I want you to see is that marriage is a covenant, not just a legal contract. It's not just an agreement of two people to live together. It's not just a bond in which they decide, ''This looks like a good thing to do.''

When two people enter into a covenant agreement, they're pledging all that they are to each other. They're coming together as one flesh, and they're coming together to set up a memorial to be a testimony to the world.

11

Covenant Commitment

Deuteronomy 32:30 asks, **"How could one chase a thousand, and two put ten thousand to flight...?"** In the covenant agreement that is made in marriage, the power of God is multiplied in your lives. God's power is multiplied in your relationship, particularly when you walk in agreement and in harmony with each other.

In Matthew 18:19-20 (AMP) the Lord says:

> **Again I tell you, if two of you on earth agree (harmonize together, together make a symphony) about — anything and everything — whatever they shall ask, it will come to pass and be done for them by My Father in heaven.**
>
> **For wherever two or three are gathered (drawn together as My followers) in (into) My name, there I AM in the midst of them.**

That's not just mental agreement. It's not just physically touching and saying, "I agree with you." The real agreement is spiritual agreement where two people are in harmony in their spirits. There's no greater possibility of power of agreement than in the marriage union. Why? Because there's no two people on earth who can get any closer in their spirits than a man and a woman who are walking in unity with God.

Now, if you understand what great power there is in a married couple being in unity, you'll understand why the devil fights marriage so hard. Marriage represents the greatest form of power possible when two people touch and agree and pray together. In this kind of agreement, Jesus said, "It will be done."

This is the kind of covenant commitment we're looking for from the marriages in our church. Multiplied power, ten times that which each has as an individual, is granted to those who come together in agreement.

You may be thinking, "I don't know if the person I'm living with right now is the right one for me." Well, if you're married to that individual, they are the right one! You're in covenant agreement. You're a covenant believer in covenant relationship.

One of the things that we need to decide concerning marriage is that *it is for life.* We're married for life. Sharon and I don't have an alternative. We've set our sights on the fact that whatever difficulties may arise, we'll work them out.

If you're married, you have to make up your mind that whatever difficulties may arise, you'll seek God's help and wisdom to find the solutions to those challenges and make that marriage relationship work. You'll believe God for the wisdom or you'll go somewhere for help to make that marriage relationship the best it can be.

When two people commit themselves to each other, the vows they make are sealed with the sign of a covenant: *an unending circle,* which is symbolized by the ring. It goes around, and once it goes around, it goes around again. It never ends. This symbolizes God's intent for marriage: *that there be an unending circle of love in the relationship.*

When two people commit their lives to each other, it's not a one-night stand. It's not a one-week deal. It's not an every-now-and-then relationship. It's a commitment that says, "I will be with you for the rest of my life." In this setting, God declares that the marriage bed is holy, honorable, and undefiled. (Heb. 13:4.)

12

The Marriage Act

I'll refer to the physical union between the husband and wife (what the world calls "sex") as "the marriage act," because that's where it belongs. God intended the physical act of sex to be performed only in the marriage, flowing through a bond of love.

The marriage union, as God designed it, is something very beautiful, holy, honorable, and wonderful. It's a place where the husband and wife can freely express their love for one another at the deepest level, not just surface level, but spirit, soul, and body. It's a place where they can say to the person to whom they've committed their whole life: "I love you, and I give the totality of myself to you." Nothing is withheld.

Hebrews 13:4 says that the marriage bed is to be undefiled: **Marriage is honorable among all, and the bed undefiled; but fornicators and adulterers God** *will judge.* The *marriage bed* has to do with the sexual act of marriage. God is saying, "The sexual act in marriage is to be honorable, holy, and undefiled."

When you talk with a lot of people about sex, if they don't understand what the Bible says, you can make them feel like it's dirty, wrong, and unclean. I'm *not* telling you that, because the sexual act is beautiful, holy, and honorable *in marriage.*

God's Word says, ...**but fornicators and adulterers God will judge.** Fornication is the sexual act between single people. Adultery is when two people commit the sexual act who are married (or one person is married and the other is single), but they're not married to each other. God treats fornication and adultery in the same light. In either case, there's no commitment. There's no bond of love. There's no union. There's no covenant. They're joining together in the sexual act *in violation of God's Word.*

God looks at both adultery and fornication as a violation of His laws. He says, "I will judge these people."

In the marriage union, when two people come together in the marriage act, there's no guilt, no remorse, and no fear. In contrast, when two people come together in the sexual act outside of marriage, just the opposite is true: 1) There will be a sense of guilt, because God's laws have been violated; 2) there will be remorse, because these two people aren't married and possibly may never get married in the future; and 3) there will be fear of discovery or fear that a child will be conceived out of the relationship.

All types of heaviness and oppression come on people who enter the sexual act outside of marriage.

In working with teenagers, I have seen the fear, oppression, and heaviness which come on them when they become sexually involved in a relationship before marriage. The freedom, joy, pureness, and inner peace in their lives are gone once they begin to violate God's laws. Commit yourself to stay pure before God.

13

Unconditional Love

**But God demonstrates His own love toward us,
in that while we were still sinners, Christ died for us.**

Romans 5:8

Unconditional love is that ...**while we were still
sinners, Christ died for us.** This means that we didn't do
anything to cause God to love us. We did not solicit, draw
out, or create the love that He showed toward us. His love
was already in Him, and His love flowed out toward us,
not because of what we did, but *in spite of what we did* —
not because of what we were, but *in spite of what we were.*
God's unconditional love flowed out, not just to you, but
to every human being on the earth.

Jesus introduced a new type of love, the God-kind of
love. A phrase that describes the God-kind of love is
unconditional love. It isn't based upon what you can get out
of a relationship, but it's based on something that God has
done in you. God puts His love inside of you, and you love
because love is in you. To describe this to the world is
impossible. It is beyond human comprehension, because
the love in the world is based upon getting, gaining, or
grabbing. It's based upon, "If you'll do something, I'll love
you. If you're nice, I'll love you."

...**while we were still sinners, Christ died for us.**
Christ loved us even when we were unlovable.

Dave Roever, a Viet Nam veteran who survived the
explosion of a phosphorus hand grenade that blew off a
great portion of his face, shared his testimony with our

congregation. He told how the wife of the man in the hospital bed next to his took her wedding ring off when she looked at the person she couldn't even recognize as her husband, saying, "It's all over."

Dave, fearful because of this blatant rejection, shared how his wife walked in the room and checked his name tag, because she was unable to identify him as the man she had married a few months earlier.

He said to her, "Honey, I don't look very pretty now." She laughed and said, "Davey, you never did look very pretty!" She then reached down and kissed him on that burned flesh. To this day, she's still with him. Now, that's unconditional love. That's the God-kind of love. Why? Because she made a commitment that went beyond what he looked like or what the circumstances were.

God has called us to unconditional love, and the only way we can have that kind of love is when God comes inside of our hearts through Jesus Christ. When He lives inside of us, then that kind of love can be in us so we can love our brothers, sisters, mother, father, mate, and others.

Unconditional love begins by receiving love in your heart, and God is that love! Love comes in your heart by invitation:

> **"Behold, I stand at the door** (of your heart) **and knock. If anyone hears My voice and opens the door, I will come in to him and dine with him, and he with Me."**

> **Revelation 3:20**

Unconditional love is a Person. It may be a term we use to describe something, but He (the Lord Jesus Christ) is the love that God showed.

> **"For God so loved the world that He gave His only begotten Son, that whoever believes in Him should not perish but have everlasting life."**

> **John 3:16**

This love isn't just for those who pass the entrance exam, nor for those who can jump the highest or look the best. It's for "whoever will believe in Him." That's the only requirement for receiving His unconditional love.

Some of the definitions of *unconditional* are "perfect, absolute, complete, whole, unlimited, positive, certain, real, and unfailing." Unconditional love is a healthy respect and trust of others as persons of worth and value. This is the kind of love that God has for us, and this is the kind of love we need to have for others as we represent Christ in our marriages, in our families and homes, in our church families, and in the marketplace.

14
Four Types of Love

Many times as people hear us begin to talk about love, it's misinterpreted, because we might say, "I love to ride horses," or "I love to go to ball games," or "I love popcorn." Then we turn to our wife and say, "I love you."

There is a love, an appreciation, an affection, and an enjoyment that we get out of all of these things, but the problem in the English language is that we've used the same word for all of it. So when we come to someone and say, "I love you," in many cases, it doesn't carry the impact it should because we don't have the proper understanding of love. We have watered down the word *love* to the point it no longer carries the meaning that it should to people.

We should guard how we use the word *love* so when it is used it carries the meaning and the power God intended when we speak it.

In the Greek language, there are four words for *love: agape, phileo, eros,* and *astorgos.* When someone says, "I love you," any one of four things could be meant.

Agape

First, we'll talk about *agape,* a Greek word for *love,* which means "the God-kind of love" or "unconditional love" that we just talked about. John 3:16 is an example of *agape* love.

Agape love is self-giving. It gives out of itself. *Agape* love wants to benefit the other person. In other words, Jesus suffered on the cross, not for His own benefit, but for *our* benefit. That's the way *agape* love is: *it will sacrifice itself to benefit the other person.*

Everything First Corinthians 13 says about love is descriptive of *agape*, the God-kind of love:

1. It is longsuffering.
2. It is kind.
3. It doesn't envy or parade itself.
4. It isn't puffed up.
5. It doesn't behave itself rudely.
6. It doesn't seek its own.
7. It isn't easily provoked.
8. It thinks no evil.
9. It doesn't rejoice in iniquity, but rejoices in the truth.
10. It bears all things.
11. It believes all things.
12. It hopes all things.
13. It endures all things.
14. It never fails.

Agape love will never abuse another person. It will hurt itself to avoid hurting someone else. *Agape* love will give of itself, even if there is hurt and pain.

Agape love will not give up on the other person. If you are praying and believing for the restoration of a relationship, let me encourage you: *God's love won't fail.* If you operate according to God's Word, His love will not fail. You have a choice to believe God or believe your own feelings.

God never allows His love for us to come to an end. He never divorces us. Thank God He doesn't. Feed into your subconscious, "I'm going to make this marriage work." If you have a determination to make your marriage work, God will make it work.

W. E. Vine said that love can be known only from the action that it prompts.[1] John 13:34,35 supports this word from W. E. Vine.

"**A new commandment I give to you, that you love one another; as I have loved you, that you also love one another.**

"**By this all will know that you are My disciples, if you have love for one another.**"

Phileo

The second Greek work for *love* is *phileo*. The word *phileo* deals with affection or friendship in the soulish realm. It has a lot to do with the fellowship aspect of love. It's a high kind of love. It's not as high as *agape*, but *phileo* is a *brotherly type of love*. It's love on the human level — the highest form of love that humanity can reach without Christ.

The true meaning of the word *agape* was really introduced by Jesus. It was a word that captured love that was beyond human love. Brotherly love will do a lot of things, but it will never go to the extent of *agape* love.

One time when we were driving, Sharon said to me, "You know, you're not only my lover, but you're my best friend." God calls us in a marriage relationship not only to be lovers, but to be friends, relating those things in life that are important and valuable.

Phileo love is a love that consists of whatever we see in another person that gives us pleasure. Even people who aren't saved can experience *phileo* love. They can see something in another person that gives pleasure, that's enjoyable, and that's delightful. Their love, attraction, and the drawing between them is based upon what's seen and can be developed into a friendship relationship.

---

[1] W.E. Vine, *Vine's Expository Dictionary of Old and New Testament Words* (Old Tappan: Fleming H. Revell Company, 1981), Vol. III, p. 21.

Eros

The third Greek word for *love* is *eros*. The word *erotic* comes from *eros*, which is a physical love. *Eros* has to do with a sensual type of attraction — a love not based upon self-giving, but based upon *self-serving* and *self-receiving*. *Eros* wants for itself. It wants to get rather than give. *Eros will sacrifice another person to satisfy itself.*

In contrast, *agape* will sacrifice itself to benefit another person, while *eros* will use a person to satisfy its own selfish desires and lusts. *Eros* and lust flow together, because they both have to do with a physical, sensual type of love.

Astorgos

Astorgos love has to do with affection. Examples of this type of love are patting a child on the head, a grandmother showing affection to her grandchild, or you showing love to an elderly relative. In many cases, *astorgos* love has no depth or commitment to it.

All four of these types of love find their beauty and expression in the marriage relationship in which there is no perversion, but rather a beautiful release and flow of God's Spirit.

The world is looking for the love of God. It's looking for a real love, and so many times the world has received a counterfeit. Satan has a counterfeit for everything that God has, and the devil's kind of love is a perversion. He perverts the *eros* kind of love, the physical love. This kind of love is pleasurable only for a season. The pleasure of it stops after a while. It can't go on. It's not eternal, but *agape* love is eternal.

Once you have *agape* love, including all the other types of love within it, you'll have a beautiful balanced life and relationship as husband and wife.

15

Love in the Marriage and Family

First Corinthians 13 in *The Amplified Bible* gives a good description of the love God has designed for all of our relationships. This portion of Scripture describes the *agape*, unconditional, or God-kind of love.

If I [can] speak in the tongues of men and [even] of angels, but have not love [that reasoning, intentional, spiritual devotion such as is inspired by God's love for and in us], I am only a noisy gong or a clanging cymbal.

And if I have prophetic powers — that is, the gift of interpreting the divine will and purpose; and understand all the secret truths and mysteries and possess all knowledge, and if I have (sufficient) faith so that I can remove mountains, but have not love [God's love in me] I am nothing — a useless nobody.

Even if I dole out all that I have [to the poor in providing] food, and if I surrender my body to be burned [or in order that I may glory], but have not love [God's love in me], I gain nothing.

Love endures long and is patient and kind; love never is envious nor boils over with jealousy; is not boastful or vainglorious, does not display itself haughtily.

It is not conceited — arrogant and inflated with pride; it is not rude (unmannerly) and does not act unbecomingly. Love [God's love in us] does not insist on its own rights or its own way, for it is not self-seeking; it is not touchy or fretful or resentful; it takes

no account of the evil done to it — pays no attention to a suffered wrong.

It does not rejoice at injustice and unrighteousness, but rejoices when right and truth prevail.

1 Corinthians 13:1-6 AMP

In other words, when there's sin or shortcoming, injustice, and unrighteousness, love doesn't gloat over it. Love isn't delighted in it. Instead, there's often an inner grieving when that happens.

Love rejoices when right and truth prevail. Sometimes, people (particularly Christians) get caught up in reading the bad reports about other people. I don't care to hear a bad report about you or about anyone else. I'm not rejoicing in something that's being trumped up as wrong. I rejoice when right and truth prevail.

It's the same way in our lives. You and I should never allow ourselves to rejoice inwardly or delightfully or entertain thoughts about another Christian's shortcomings and failures. Love reaches out to pray for that individual and stands in the gap for them.

Sometimes I think there should be by-laws for in-laws. One of them should be, ''Never listen to your in-laws (or anyone else) criticize, ridicule, or belittle your mate,'' because if you do, it will be a poison inside of your relationship that will bring forth a harvest of evil in days to come.

How many relationships have been poisoned because seeds of destruction were born inside of that marriage relationship when someone pointed out the faults and failures and was critical of a mate?

Love bears up under anything and everything that comes, is ever ready to believe the best of every person, its hopes are fadeless under all circumstances, and it endures everything [without weakening].

1 Corinthians 13:7 AMP

One of the greatest things about love is that it's always ready to believe the best of every person. In the marriage relationship, we need to believe the best of the other person. Don't be suspicious of your mate about what they said or the way they said it, what they did or did not do, but be willing to give them the benefit of the doubt. They are innocent until proven guilty, and if they are guilty, you're going to forgive them.

Believing the best of every person means they're innocent. Don't go on the basis that they're guilty until proven innocent. Go on the basis that they're innocent, and if they're proven guilty, you'll minister love to them.

Love never brings up the faults of another person. It covers the faults, and there's an element of confronting one another and speaking the truth in love, which we'll talk about when we talk about communication.

Love never fails — never fades out or becomes obsolete or comes to an end. As for prophecy [that is, the gift of interpreting the divine will and purpose], it will be fulfilled and pass away; as for tongues, they will be destroyed and cease; as for knowledge, it will pass away [that is, it will lose its value and be superseded by truth].

For our knowledge is fragmentary (incomplete and imperfect), and our prophecy (our teaching) is fragmentary (incomplete and imperfect).

But when the complete and perfect [total] comes, the incomplete and imperfect will vanish away — become antiquated, void, and superseded.

When I was a child, I talked like a child, I thought like a child, I reasoned like a child; now that I have become a man, I am done with childish ways and have put them aside.

For now we are looking in a mirror that gives only a dim (blurred) reflection [of reality as in a riddle or enigma], but then [when perfection comes] we shall

see in reality and face to face! Now I know in part (imperfectly); but then I shall know and understand fully and clearly, even in the same manner as I have been fully and clearly known and understood [by God].

And so faith, hope, love abide; [faith, conviction and belief respecting man's relation to God and divine things; hope, joyful and confident expectation of eternal salvation; love, true affection for God and man, growing out of God's love for and in us], these three, but the greatest of these is love.

1 Corinthians 13:8-13 AMP

16

Finding the Right Mate

Successful Christian marriages are made out of successful Christian individuals. When you find two individuals who are walking in success in the light of God's Word, and God brings them together, then there will most likely be harmony after they get married.

It doesn't matter how good-looking someone is, how much money they have, or any other natural thing that they might possess. If they're not walking in harmony with God and with their fellow man, they're not going to be able to walk in harmony once they get married.

I believe it's time for us as parents and leaders to encourage people to set the highest standards by, first of all, setting the highest standards for ourselves and for our own walk with God. You may be thinking, "What is the highest standard?" The highest standard is given in God's Word.

In Matthew 6:33 Jesus says, **"But seek first the kingdom of God and His righteousness, and all these things shall be added to you."** In this setting, Jesus is teaching about the Gentiles or those who aren't serving God but who are seeking after money, clothes, and houses. Their lives are set on gaining things. But Jesus says, "Don't seek for these things, because if you'll seek first the Kingdom of God and His righteousness, all of these things will be added unto you."

This same principle works in marriage. When you seek God first, God will bring to you the very best person that you could marry. When you put God first, you'll be in the right place to meet the right person and establish the right relationship that will produce success in marriage.

Often, people seek after a mate, but the Bible says to seek after God. As you seek Him first, He'll bring you into contact with the right individual. He'll bring you in contact with someone who is also seeking God.

17

The Dating Scene

God gives us a clear-cut admonition not to be unequally yoked together with unbelievers:

Do not be unequally yoked together with unbelievers. For what fellowship has righteousness with lawlessness? And what communion has light with darkness?

And what accord has Christ with Belial? Or what part has a believer with an unbeliever?

And what agreement has the temple of God with idols? For you are the temple of the living God. As God has said: *"I will dwell in them and walk among them. I will be their God, and they shall be My people."*

Therefore *"Come out from among them and be separate, says the Lord. Do not touch what is unclean, and I will receive you."*

"I will be a Father to you, and you shall be My sons and daughters, says the Lord Almighty."

2 Corinthians 6:14-18

If you begin to date an unbeliever and become involved in a friendship relationship leading toward the possibility of marriage, just remember: *every date doesn't end in marriage, but every marriage begins with a date.*

It's a possibility that in dating a Canaanite you might fall in love with a Canaanite. The Bible is very clear in the Old Testament concerning this. There was to be no joining together between the inhabitants of the land of Canaan and the children of Israel. Once the Israelites trespassed God's commandment, there was a gradual infiltration of the worship of idols in the place of the worship of God.

God has a purpose for a believer not uniting with an unbeliever. He wants a strong union that can be a testimony to the world. There are many people today who married unbelievers thinking their mates would change after marriage, and they've suffered years and years of heartache. You need to teach your sons and daughters this Biblical principle and establish it in them.

We do not reject unbelievers or put them down, but we're not to be joined to unbelievers in marriage. Instead, we're to pray for them to come to a knowledge of Christ.

When two people want to get married, some of the first questions I ask them are: Do you know if your mate is saved? Do they pray in the Spirit? Do they read their Bible? Do they fellowship with God? Do they have to be nudged by you to get involved in the things of God, or are they motivated on their own?

When someone is looking for a mate, they need to look for someone who is self-motivated to seek God, because if they have to be pumped every time they are to seek God, that'll quickly wear out and will become a source of contention. You need to look for a person to date who has already made a choice to serve God, whether they marry you or not.

Witnessing —
An Excuse for Dating an Unbeliever

Sometimes young people use the excuse of "a need to witness" to an unbeliever as their justification for dating them. I've got news for you. You can witness to someone without dating them. I've heard that excuse and seen the negative results of it too many times.

Years ago, Sharon prayed with a young woman at an altar who had been dating an unbeliever with the attitude that she was going to witness to him and bring him closer to the Lord.

After two or three months of dating, these young people fell in love with each other and then decided they were going to get married. But the young woman came to the altar one night, because her spirit was grieved. She was crying inside, because she knew her fiance wasn't saved.

Although they had already decided to get married, Sharon told her, "You're not locked into this thing yet, even though you may have announced your engagement. It may be a week, a day, or the very day of the wedding, but you're not locked into it yet. You can change it."

Then Sharon asked, "What have you witnessed to him?" She said, "I've been waiting for the right moment."

Sharon replied, "You've waited too long!"

This young woman was trapped by the devil into a relationship where her intention was right in the beginning, but she felt she couldn't get out of it. She didn't want to offend the person by witnessing to him, yet she realized the relationship was not right.

Many times people think they're going to witness, and they keep waiting for that right moment. In the meantime, they begin to fall in love with the unbeliever, and it's dangerous.

We are a righteous seed, and God wants to bring salvation to others in this earth through us, but it's not going to happen through believers dating unbelievers. When you begin to date someone, you accept everything about that person.

You don't necessarily have to date a lot of people to be successful in marriage. Dating is not a required demand. I've been around a number of people who have gone through the whole dating scene, and they came to a point of saying, "You know, this whole thing is just a rat race.

It's just a game." They've been hurt and disappointed so many times. Finally they say, "I'm going to let God lead me to the person I'm going to marry." This, of course, puts them in position to receive "God's best" in a mate.

Single Versus Group Dating

If you're a teenager, I want to encourage you to group date or double date. Dating is a Westernized cultural activity (it's not mentioned once in the Bible), and is meant to be a time for fellowship, character development, and social development. If you're in a "friend" relationship with another person of the opposite sex, there are things in your life that can be developed through dating. But if the purpose is truly for character development, fellowship, and friendship, then there's no problem with other people being present.

When I first went to Oral Roberts University, group dating was totally foreign to me. I had never heard of it. Instead of just two people going somewhere, when they got ready to go skating or do something, a whole group of young people went. It wasn't always just couples. Sometimes there were five or six guys and seven or eight girls. In other words, we all went together and began to experience relationships without this phony, plastic dating mentality. The relationships were genuine. It was an opportunity to be a friend.

Many young people don't know another boy or girl as friends. They only know boys and girls as dating objects. You need to have a relationship where you can just be friends with people of the opposite sex in which you can communicate without being involved in some heavy type of thing.

Avoid being alone with just one person of the opposite sex. The greatest temptations come when two people are alone in a parked car when there's a full moon and the breeze is blowing through the trees. When a young woman says, ''Oh, God, please help me,'' it's probably a little late for her to ask for His help.

Avoid those times alone on the beach or in a park. You may be thinking, ''Are you kidding?'' No, I'm very serious. You're totally deceived if you think the devil won't tempt you when you're alone with a young lady or a young man and it's a beautiful night.

I mean, the devil has been at this thing for a while, and he knows how to set up a scene to move on your emotions and your desires to get you overwhelmed to do things that aren't right. The best thing to do is stay out of these situations.

Double dating, groups, and fellowships are beautiful, and we need to have as many of them as possible to give young people the fellowship they need with other people their age. But the thing about single dating is that it opens the door to the devil. I don't care how strong a Christian is as a junior high or high school student, they need the strength and protection of the Lord by having other people with them.

We've been so programmed by the world that we've felt like we had to single date just because it's what everyone else is doing. We don't have to do it because everyone else is doing it. God says we're a peculiar people. People in the world don't understand why we act the way we do, but that's all right. It's just that we know how to protect ourselves.

18
Deceived and Defiled

I want to address an area that when I was growing up we called "making out, petting, or necking," which is the sexual arousal or stimulation of another person caused by touching or being involved in a heavy, making-out scene.

In marriage, these things are designed to bring a husband and wife to the point where they can flow in harmony and unity in the marriage act. With teenagers who aren't married, however, what often happens is they get into the touching process, which is like a stack of dominoes that are lined up, one behind the other. You push the first one down, and they all fall down. It's like a time bomb with a long fuse on it.

When you get into a heavy, making-out scene, you light the fuse. The fuse burns for a while, and then you say, "We've got to stop." You put the fuse out or try to put it out. Maybe you do. Maybe you don't. Then, on the next date, this same process is repeated. Maybe what was exciting to you or the other person on the last date is no longer as exciting, so you go further, and as you go further, the fuse burns a little longer.

The brakes are thrown on, but everything inside of the human body is moving one direction. God made the man and the woman to flow from the sexual stimulation of one another all the way through to the marriage act.

Here's where the tremendous emotional frustration comes in young men and women. They start into heavy petting, and then suddenly, it's stopped. Everything inside of them is twisted up mentally, emotionally, and physically.

People who carry on this type of relationship let the fuse burn a little longer. What happens to many people is they don't realize how short the fuse has gotten, and suddenly, that bomb goes off! They aren't able to stop what was begun way back at the beginning.

I want you to see the whole process of understanding marriage and God's purpose in it and how God made the man and the woman to physically come together, not out of obligation, but out of real joy and pleasure. Then you can understand what a violation it is to get into the marriage act while you're dating (no matter what your age). It's a violation of the way God made you. It's a violation of your own body.

You may be asking, "Well, what should I do?" I'm glad you asked. *Don't ever light the fuse until you're under the covering protection of marriage to start and finish what you've begun.* That's when the fuse should be lit.

Defilement Begins in the Heart

And He (Jesus) said, "What comes out of a man, that defiles a man.

"For from within, out of the heart of men, proceed evil thoughts, adulteries, fornications, murders."

Mark 7:20,21

Jesus puts adulteries and fornications side by side. I've been shocked to hear young people say, "Well, God's against adultery, but it's okay if you have sex before marriage." They fail to comprehend that in God's eyes, adultery and fornication are one and the same.

Jesus goes on:

"thefts, covetousness, wickedness, deceit, licentiousness (the *King James Version* says "lasciviousness"), an evil eye, blasphemy, pride, foolishness.

"All these evil things come from within and defile a man."

Mark 7:22,23

Lasciviousness is a word you probably don't use every day. It means "the tendency to be excited sexually in your mind," through pornography, evil imaginations, necking, making out, petting, and that whole scene. It excites and stimulates a person sexually outside of the bonds of marriage. Jesus said, "These things come out of the heart of man."

Because of the availability of pornography today in movies, TV, videos, and magazines, people can easily get into lasciviousness, sensuality, and concupiscence, which is a spirit of uncleanness. You can get into it without even being in a relationship with another young man or woman.

In First Corinthians 6:9 the Apostle Paul says, **Do you not know that the unrighteous will not inherit the kingdom of God?** *Do not be deceived....*

This is the deception of millions of young people today. They think they're going to get into heaven doing certain things. Paul says, "Don't be deceived. The unrighteous will *not* inherit the Kingdom of God." Then He names the areas of unrighteousness:

...**Neither fornicators** (those who commit sex before marriage), **nor idolaters** (those who make an idol and put it ahead of God), **nor adulterers, nor homosexuals** (the *King James Version* says "effeminate" instead of homosexuals, but they are one and the same), **nor sodomites,**

nor thieves, nor covetous, nor drunkards, nor revilers, nor extortioners will inherit the kingdom of God.

And such were some of you. But you were washed, but you were sanctified, but you were justified in the name of the Lord Jesus and by the Spirit of our God.

1 Corinthians 6:9-11

Such Were Some of You

Paul was talking to the believers at Corinth when he said, **And such were some of you....** The good news is that they were washed, sanctified, and justified in the name of Jesus and by the Spirit of God.

If you've been involved in some of these areas, don't condemn yourself saying, "There's no hope for my life." When you repent and turn from sin and you are justified, sanctified, and redeemed, you become a part of the Body of Christ.

Paul said:

All things are lawful for me, but all things are not helpful. All things are lawful for me, but *I will not be brought under the power of any*.

Foods for the stomach and the stomach for foods, but God will destroy both it and them. Now the body is not for sexual immorality but for the Lord, and the Lord for the body.

And God both raised up the Lord and will also raise us up by His power.

Do you not know that your bodies are members of Christ? Shall I then take the members of Christ and make them members of a harlot? Certainly not!

Or do you not know that he who is joined to a harlot is one body with her? For *"The two,"* He says, *"shall become one flesh."*

But he who is joined to the Lord is one spirit with Him.

1 Corinthians 6:12-17

I believe these next three verses were written particularly for teenagers, but the principle applies to any age:

Flee sexual immorality. Every sin that a man does is outside the body, but he who commits sexual immorality sins against his own body.

Or do you not know that your body is the temple of the Holy Spirit who is in you, whom you have from God, and you are not your own?

For you were bought at a price; therefore glorify God in your body and in your spirit, which are God's.
1 Corinthians 6:18-20

19
Hold On to Your Virginity!

When a young woman gives herself to a young man physically outside of the bonds of marriage, she has no promise or commitment from that young man. I've seen many young women disappointed in this type of situation of being free with their own bodies. Then they come to the point of wanting to get married and they say, "I want to give myself totally to the young man I'm going to marry."

The only problem is: *they don't have anything to give, because they've already given themselves.* When they come to that moment where they want to be beautiful and holy and they want to be able to say, "I'm giving all of myself to you," they don't have all of themselves to give. It's gone. It's called *virginity!*

It's glorious to be a virgin, whether you're a young man or a young woman, when coming into the marriage relationship. It's a wonderful moment to be able to say to that person: "I am all yours. Everything that I am belongs to you. I give myself to you without reserve."

If you've been violated or you've violated another person, cleansing is available through the blood of Jesus Christ. There's a cleansing by the power of the Holy Spirit that can make you new and give you the power to be able to say "no," either to end a wrong relationship or to keep you from ever entering into a wrong relationship.

20

Make Plans for Marriage in Your Teen Years

Sharon and I were in three different seminars on marriage and the family while we were engaged. We read a lot of books on marriage and family relationships. We talked with couples, and we asked them, "What have you done that has made your marriage successful, or what do you wish you had done that would have made it better?"

When you seek for wisdom, God will give it to you. Some men will spend hours working on their golf putt or on their back swing to drive that little white ball down the middle of the fairway or make it roll straight onto the green. They'll watch the pros play on Saturday and Sunday afternoon and they'll read *Golf Digest*, but they won't take 15 minutes to read a good book that would make their marriage more successful.

In a sense, you can treat going into marriage in the same way you would treat going into a profession. You get out of anything what you put into it. If you put something into marriage and into the preparation for a family, then you can have the greatest family and the greatest marriage in the whole world! It can be an example to other people.

I began to question, "What's going to yield the greatest degree of happiness in my life?" Many times we'll spend four years or more and several thousand dollars to get a degree to enter a career that we may change after a year or two.

When you enter into a marriage relationship, it's seven days a week, twenty-four hours a day. You should have a greater degree of commitment to make your marriage, home, and family successful than any other thing, whether business, recreation, or study.

Sometimes people have the attitude, "I've lived in a family all of my life. I know all there is to know about a family." You can go to a grocery store and spend a lot of time there, but you may not know all there is to know about all of its products. We can use that analogy in many things. Just because a person is married or has lived in a family doesn't mean they know beans about a family or about a marriage, because many of the things we've learned from others and from the world are erroneous.

We need to go to God's Word and to those who have studied God's Word and have become teachers in the area of marriage, family, and the home to seek their counsel.

Sharon can always tell when I've read a good book on marriage. I really get motivated! I'm in there plugging away and washing dishes after I've read one of those books. She would like for me to read all of the time, because it has a definite effect upon me! We still go to marriage seminars. We don't feel that we've arrived just because we've had training. There are still areas in which we can improve.

We're talking about getting the most out of your relationship, about having the maximum joy and peace and love that there can be in your marriage, your home, and your family.

Too many young people settle for mediocrity in marriage, and a lot of people haven't even hit mediocre yet. They say, "This may not be too good, but at least we're still married." That doesn't go for me. Whatever I do, I want it to be productive, and I want it to be a blessing and be fruit-bearing. That's the attitude that you should have toward your relationship (or toward your prospective marriage relationship).

It's never too early to start learning about how to have a godly marriage, because you're being shaped, even as a teenager. The attitudes and character traits that are being developed in teen years will come out in marriage down the road.

I think young people ought to start planning for marriage when they're thirteen — thinking about being the kind of person someone else would want to live with, developing the right personality and the good character traits, and learning how to have a good family, a better home, and a happy marriage.

21
Children
Are the Heritage
of the Lord

Behold, children are a heritage from the Lord, The fruit of the womb is His reward.

Psalm 127:3

In other words, children are a reward from God.

Like arrows in the hand of a warrior, So are the children of one's youth.

Psalm 127:4

What does a mighty man do with arrows? He shoots them against an enemy. It's God's plan that a godly seed be raised up to destroy the works of the enemy. God said that children are as arrows in the hand of a mighty man.

Happy is the man who has his quiver full of them; They shall not be ashamed, But shall speak with their enemies in the gate.

Psalm 127:5

Gate represents "a place of authority." The godly seed who are being raised up will deal with the enemy in the place of authority. God has called for children to be raised up as godly seed who will deal with the enemy in these last days.

Blessed is every one who fears the Lord, Who walks in His ways.

When you eat the labor of your hands,
You shall be happy, and it shall be well with you.
Your wife shall be like a fruitful vine
In the very heart of your house,
Your children like olive plants
All around your table.
Behold, thus shall the man be blessed
Who fears the Lord.
The Lord bless you out of Zion,
And may you see the good of Jerusalem
All the days of your life.
Yes, may you see your children's children . . . .

Psalm 128:1-6

Children are a heritage, a reward, arrows or weapons that will be used against the enemy in the days ahead. They are a blessing from the Lord.

22

Children Are Receptive
to the Things of God

Most children are open, receptive, and have very little pride or religiosity about them. They are usually free of doubt, unbelief, and mental hang-ups about receiving Christ.

In our apartment outreach crusades, we generally have more children than adults, and there are usually more children saved than adults. There's a reason: *for of such is the Kingdom of God.* (Matt. 19:14.) Children are easier to reach. If you tell them Jesus died for them, most of them will receive Him gladly. If you tell an adult that Jesus died for them, often they'll say, "Let me think about it. I'm not ready yet. I'm not into that stuff."

One time when Sharon and I were ministering in Florida, we took time out to go fishing. We purchased a $5.99 rod and reel from Wal-Mart, one of those little short jobs! We were right beside some men with their expensive fishing gear who weren't catching a thing. Sharon dropped the line from that short pole into the water and soon had a big barracuda on the end of it!

She started screaming and reeling it in. I was trying to find the camera so we'd have living proof that it did happen. It fell back into the water, but I can vouch that it did really happen. The moral of the story is that little children are easier to catch for the Gospel than adults!

Dwight L. Moody, a great man of God of years past, was once asked how many people were saved in a particular meeting. He said, "Three and a half." Someone asked, "Oh, you had a child saved?" He said, "No, I had three children and one adult! The adult's life is half gone."

Five months after I was saved, the Lord dealt with me. "What have you ever done for anyone else?" He asked. I was sitting in my room in an athletic dorm in a state college, and I was overwhelmed with this thought. I had never done anything for anyone else. Everything had been done for me. God dealt with me to work with third graders at a boys' club, teaching them how to play basketball.

One of the reasons our church, Victory Christian Center in Tulsa, Oklahoma, is reaching out to little children and becoming involved in the children's ministry, in the bus ministry, and in crusades is because it's better to save a life and prevent a child from going wrong than it is to try to rehabilitate him later.

If you reach children at a young age, you can see their lives continue to grow in God.

23

Train Up a Child

Train up a child in the way he should go, And when he is old he will not depart from it.

Proverbs 22:6

To *train* has to do with discipline. It means "to teach or tell, to show or demonstrate, to lead someone through the process in which they are being trained."

Training also has to do with making a person do a requested task. In other words, seeing that it's done. One part of the training process is to tell someone what they need to do. But there's also the showing of "how" to do it, leading them through it, actually going through the process and making them do it.

If you were ever in the military, you weren't told, "I want to tell you a few things and if you want to do them, that's fine. If you don't, we'll just go with the flow." No! You were told, "This is what you are going to do." If you didn't do it as directed, you were corrected. That's training. *Training makes a demand and then enforces it.*

A lie has crept into some families in the discipline area: don't make children do anything they don't want to do.

There may be things that children and young people may not like to do, but just because they don't like to do it doesn't mean we're not supposed to make them do it. I'm praying for a strengthening of backbone in moms and dads to make children do what's right, because there has developed a spirit of rebellion which has allowed children to rule and dominate their parents, to make parents bow to what they want.

God is telling us as parents to train our children, and that means not only telling them, showing them, and leading them through what we want them to do, but also making them do it.

Ephesians 6:4 says we're to ...**bring them up in the training and admonition of the Lord.** This means to bring them up in the nurture, training, discipline, and instruction of the Lord.

Proverbs 13:24 says, **He who spares his rod hates his son, but he who loves him disciplines him promptly.** This verse is saying that not to discipline your children is to hate them, but if you love them, you'll discipline them promptly.

Proverbs 19:18 says, **Chasten your son while there is hope, and do not set your heart on his destruction.**

You may be questioning, ''How long should I still use the rod on my children?'' As long as they need it! Some of the junior high school girls at Victory Christian School were talking, and one was embarrassed because she had received a spanking at home. One of the other girls asked, ''Do you still get them?'' Then she said, ''I do, too.'' Another girl said, ''I do, too. I didn't think anyone my age got them.''

I used to scream a yellow streak when Mom started to spank me. I don't know if she knew these scriptures or not, but she sure practiced them! Often, when children begin to cry, parents allow the crying to cause them to back off of the discipline and correction.

I want to clarify that we're talking about disciplining in love, because there's been a spirit that has come into the world's system, even in Christian circles, that has either done away with all discipline or has perverted it into child abuse.

The pendulum has swung to both sides: total abuse, or a total lack of discipline and correction. There's a balance in discipline for children in which there's no abuse and no lack of correction.

Proverbs 22:15 says, **Foolishness is bound up in the heart of a child, but the rod of correction will drive it far from him.** This implies that foolishness goes out of a child when he (or she) is disciplined.

Proverbs 23:13,14 (NIV) says,

> **Do not withhold discipline from a child; If you punish him with the rod, he will not die. Punish him with the rod and save his soul from death.**

Your child may say he's going to die. He may yell, "You're killing me," and all that. Don't be moved by his screaming. Now, I'm not talking about abusing, wounding, destroying, or hurting a child. But God says that with proper discipline, you'll deliver his soul from hell.

24

Correction Versus Punishment

Frustration exists when the rules aren't clearly defined and consistently enforced.

Let me encourage you to use the word *correction* rather than punishment. *Correction* includes a degree of punishment, but if you punish but don't correct, you'll have to punish again. The purpose of correction is *to alter the course of a child's life.*

Proverbs 29:15 says, **The rod and reproof give wisdom, but a child left to himself brings shame to his mother.** Some people give the rod, but they don't give the reproof. Therefore, wisdom doesn't come into the child. You must correct with the rod, but you must also correct by sowing the Word of God in the heart.

The key to discipline and correction is your spirit. If you discipline or punish with hostility, anger, frustration, or in some cases even hatred, you'll input those same forces inside the child's heart. They'll pick up the spirit as much as they pick up what they feel on their behind!

Not only are your children being trained, but you, as a parent, are being trained. If you're training your children not to lose their temper, then don't lose yours while you're correcting them.

You train, not only by what you say, but by what you communicate through your spirit, your words, and your gestures.

25

Tips for the Discipline of Children

I have included only a few of the major areas of concern in the discipline of children. This list is by no means complete.

1. *Be consistent with discipline.* This is probably the biggest challenge a parent faces, but it's a key to effective discipline.

If a child knows there's going to be consistency in the discipline, then he'll stop at the boundary line set by the parents. Children need a boundary line for security. A child who has no boundaries is basically left to himself, and he runs out of control. There's no security in his life.

A boundary line for a child is like a fence or a place of protection. I remember hearing the story of a school playground which had no fence around it. The playground was located next to a busy street with cars continually whizzing by.

The children stayed close to the school building while this huge playground remained empty. School officials couldn't get the children to use it at all, because they saw all the cars whizzing by and there was no fence or barrier to protect them.

Finally, a fence was put at the edge of the property. Once the fence was up, the children played on the entire playground, because there was a boundary and they felt secure and protected.

It's the same with a child in the family. When there are boundaries of correction, a child is free to expand and release himself in development and in educational and spiritual experiences.

2. *Discipline immediately.* You have perhaps viewed a child being beaten by an angry mother or daddy, because that frustrated parent said, "I've told you 30 times not to do that, and *now* I'm going to spank you." After they've done it 30 times is not the time to correct children!

Establish the rules or boundaries. If the rules are broken, then with no anger or animosity, go to the child and say, "What was the rule? What did I tell you to do or not to do?" Explain to him what he violated, and immediately correct him.

When a parent disciplines immediately, instead of anger being instilled in the child, a bond of love will be formed in the parent-child relationship. Hug the child after you discipline him, reassuring him of your love.

If a child gets away with breaking the rules, rebellion will build in his heart and a barrier will come between child and parent. If that rebellion is not removed, the child will carry it inside and be alienated from his parents. But if there's immediate discipline when a child is small, the spirit of rebellion will have no place in him.

3. *Discipline for instant obedience.* A child can be trained to obey after the third time he is told, or he can be trained to obey after the first time. It all depends on the trainer. Your children will be disciplined upon the basis of your level of tolerance or intolerance. They will rise to a standard or they will fall to it, depending where you set it.

When Sarah was two years old, the training she received for instant obedience saved her life. She went out the front door and started running across the lawn toward a cat that was on the other side of the street. At the same time, a car was speeding down the street. Sarah, of course, had no comprehension of the approaching car, and the car didn't see her.

A neighbor across the street stepped out of her front door just as Sarah was coming to the edge of the street. She saw Sarah and yelled, "Sarah, stop." Sarah stopped immediately, and the car went flying right on by. Because of her instant obedience, Sarah's life was spared.

If children don't learn to obey parents, they will have tremendous difficulty obeying the Word of God. One summer in Minnesota I was in a conversation with a 22-year-old man. I was talking about being a doer of the Word, obeying the Word of God, and the blessings that come from obedience. He had looked at me with a blank stare all through the worship service.

Afterwards, I talked with him and he said, "You know, I grew up on a farm, and my parents never made me do anything. I just did what I wanted. I've never had to obey anyone. Whatever I felt I wanted to do, that's what I did. I can't really understand obeying God's Word."

Suddenly, the importance of training a child to instantly obey his parents hit me. A child who has been taught instant obedience to his parents will usually exercise instant obedience to God's Word when he begins to hear it. He'll be delivered from hell. He'll understand that there's a penalty for disobedience, and there's a blessing for obedience.

4. *Don't allow your child to cause a breakdown of authority between you and your mate.* There's a breakdown in authority where either a husband or a wife will not back the authority of the other. If Sharon says something, even if I don't agree with it, or if I say something and she doesn't agree with me, we back the authority of the other. If you don't, you'll have rebellion. First Samuel 15:23 says, "**...rebellion is as the sin of witchcraft....**"

If the husband and wife don't support each other, they open the door for the enemy to attack their children. Suddenly, there are all types of manifestations of evil and the parents wonder, "Where did this come in? We take our children to church every Sunday. We've done this, and we've done that." There must be unity and harmony between the husband and wife.

5. *The husband, as head of the home, should take the lead role of disciplinarian.* God set Jesus as Head of the Church, and He set the husband as head of the home. God ordained the man to be the head of the family. The husband is to take the lead and the load.

But what has happened? Because many husbands have abdicated their place of leadership, women have had to rise up and become strong. God intended for both the husband and the wife to be strong. As acclaimed speaker and author, Edwin Louis Cole said, "God created the husband and wife, not to compete, but to *complete* each other."

Sometimes, when there's a misunderstanding of the husband's or wife's role, an opening is made allowing wicked spirits to come directly into the children. In our case, Sharon and I both discipline the children, although I usually take the leadership role. There are times when it's not comfortable to discipline, but it's always expedient. Many men don't want to be the disciplinarian, either because they aren't strong enough spiritually or because they lose control of their anger too easily.

God hasn't given men a spirit of timidity. If discipline has to take place in the home, then do it. Rise up to your calling. Discipline always brings the peaceable fruit of righteousness. What happens when you don't have discipline in the home? You have the unpeaceable fruit of unrighteousness and the manifestation of wickedness.

In situations where there's no father in the home, the mother must assume the role of disciplinarian. Mom, you can do it!

26

Open Communication
With Your Children

Bill Walton, the co-founder of Holiday Inns and president of a multi-billion-dollar international corporation, came to Christ years ago through the witness and testimony of Billy Graham. In an excerpt from a powerful article he wrote, he said, "Among the most frightened and frustrated fathers to be found anywhere are some top corporate managers I know. They can skillfully negotiate a multi-national merger, but can't seem to carry on five minutes of civil conversation with a son or daughter."[1]

It's important that you never lose the ability to have conversation with your children, talking to them and letting them talk to you. This is something requiring work.

From my viewpoint, it appears that many parents can't really carry on a conversation with their children. They give them orders, they tell them what to do and what not to do, but children need a talking/listening relationship with their parents. It requires listening to get on their level.

With our little boy, Paul, he wants me to play with his little toy men, animals, and cars. When our girls were his age, they wanted me to play dolls with them. Today, I have a talking relationship with all of my children. When they're going through a problem or a difficulty or just day-to-day

---

[1]Bill Walton, "When the 'Boss' Comes Home," *Voice Magazine,* Full Gospel Business Men's Fellowship International, Publishers, P. O. Box 5050, Costa Mesa, CA 92628, Vol. 38, No. 12, Dec. 1990, p. 4.

things, they're able to openly communicate with both Sharon and me.

The question was asked in a youth group from another church, "How many of you have had your mother or father hug you and tell you 'I love you' in the last week?" Over 50 percent of the teenagers present said they hadn't been hugged or told they were loved during the previous week. It's okay to hug teenagers! It's okay to hug little children and take them in your arms and love them! If there's anything young people need today, it's the sense of security and acceptance that comes from knowing that someone loves them.

Many young people have a macho image of their father, in which case the father isn't tender nor does he represent Jesus. Young people need to remember: *your model isn't in Hollywood. It's the Son of God!* Jesus Christ is your pattern.

It takes humility to relate to your children. Ken Anderson, president of Ken Anderson Films, says, "We have found that children go astray from homes where the solemn truths of the Bible are proclaimed as dynamic law, but where parents, however sincere, fail to add that warmth of genuineness which must be seen for the Christian faith to ring real in a child's calculating mind."[2]

This man has produced Christians films for many years, and he and his wife have raised seven children. All of their children are born again, and are serving God today. He talks about the days when their children were small. The family didn't have money to stay in a hotel, so they bought a little tent. He and his wife raised their children to see that families could have fun together as Christians.

Many parents say, "I'm going to lay down the law to my children." You may lay down the law, but remember

---

[2]Ken Anderson, "The Family That Plays Together," *The Marriage Affair*, edited by J. Allan Petersen (Wheaton: Tyndale House Publishers, 1971), p. 199.

this: The letter kills, but the Spirit gives life. When there's fun in the home and laughter around the table, children see that what you believe is real.

We encountered a man in one of our crusades who had been living under a bridge for three weeks. He shared how growing up he was in a home which went to church all the time and taught all the commandments, but where there was no warmth and no love. As soon as he could get away from it, he ran as far as he could.

When there is a warm acceptance and love in the home, children won't run from Christianity. They'll desire to embrace it.

27

Goal in Discipline: Character Development

The goal in discipline and correction should be character development: training children and young people in the principles of godly character.

High on your list of what you are working to instill in your children and teenagers should be the fear of the Lord. We are living in a society today that, for the most part, doesn't have a reverential fear of God. Many things are done without a sense of reprisal or judgment. There's no sense of honor, holiness, or integrity.

As a result, lives are wrecked, because the wages of sin are death, not only in eternity, but here and now. Sin has a penalty right here on the earth. People are being destroyed because they don't know how to fear God. The fear of the Lord is to depart from evil. It is the beginning of wisdom. This must be instilled in children.

Children must be taught to respect authority. They must be taught hard work, responsibility, faithfulness, integrity, and honesty, as opposed to stealing, cheating, and lying.

When you punish without instilling godly principles into your children's lives, they may not even know why they're being punished.

Arthur Gordon, a magazine editor, said: ''Many thoughtful police officers see a direct and unmistakable connection between juvenile crime and parents who are so afraid that their children won't have everything that they deprive them of nothing. The excuse such parents often give is that they want their children 'to have the things we didn't have.' Last November, in a letter to the local newspaper, Lieutenant Robert Funk of the Savannah (Georgia) police department addressed himself to such parents.

" 'Of course we want our children to have all the things we didn't have, but what are some of these things? Our parents didn't let us stay out all night. We were not allowed to be disrespectful to people. We were not allowed to eat "junk" all the time. We were not allowed to throw our clothes around. We were not idle; we had jobs to do at home. We didn't receive money unless we earned it. We didn't enter a room without knocking on the door. We didn't fail to attend religious services...It's not too late to set down some rules,' he concluded. 'Our children are starving...for some real leadership. Help your child today, for he or she will be the citizen of tomorrow.' "[1] That's a good word from a policeman!

An effective part of character development in children is the reinforcement of the positives in their lives. Many parents, with an appropriate motive of correcting and bringing proper training, get off course by fault-finding rather than accentuating the positives.

Perfectionism will cause bitterness in children, because children aren't perfect. If you could see a video of how you acted when you were growing up, it might help your memory! You need to make allowances for the age of your children. They can't be compared with someone who is five or six years older. Find reasons to praise them in what they are doing right in their lives.

---

[1]Arthur Gordon "Demand Their Best," *The Marriage Affair*, edited by J. Allan Petersen (Wheaton: Tyndale House Publishers, 1971. Used by permission. All rights reserved.), p. 180.

Today, many children and teenagers are under oppression, because they have a barrage of accusations against them day in and day out. You can change that by speaking that which is good. It's like inflating a balloon. As the old song says, ''Accentuate the positive, eliminate the negative, latch on to the affirmative, and don't mess with Mr. In-Between!'' This doesn't mean you won't deal with negatives, but try to find something good in each of your children and make something out of it. Let praise come from your lips to your children.

You may not be able to select the profession your children choose, but you can determine the kind of character they will have in their lives. You can instill in them honesty, integrity, respect for authority, and obedience. Then no matter what profession they pursue, those qualities will benefit them.

Shake off fear concerning the destiny of your children. Build your faith to believe, speak, and see that they're going to make it, victoriously, walking in obedience to God.

You should have minimum goals for your children to be saved, filled with the Holy Spirit, involved in a local church, and fruitful and productive for the Kingdom of God.

The more you want of your children, the more you must be willing to invest in them. It will take prayer, time, and faith. With children, love is spelled T-I-M-E!

Men have often made a god of their work so they have little or no time for their families. Women have also allowed work and the desire to make more money to keep them from being with their children.

Single parents have no choice. One of the most difficult situations we face in our apartment outreach crusades is that of single parents with three or four children. As a parent (whether married or single), you have a calling to raise your children, to train them, and to put inside of them what needs to be instilled in them. A new car this year may not be as important as your children serving God 25 years down the road.

We live in a materialistic society that has pressed people for more and more things. One day those things will be gone, but when your children rise up and bless you because you invested time in them, that will be worth all the things that you may have sacrificed.

Many men are working two and three jobs with extended hours just for extra "things." The family might prefer to have Dad home a few more hours! You should never sacrifice the Word or your family in order to make money. Put the Word and prayer first, your family second, then work and study.

I'm not always involved as far as being present in everything that's going on at Victory Christian Center, because there are commitments I've made to be with my family. When I first started in ministry, I let the work snowball in my life. I felt a sense of obligation to be in every meeting. The day came that a change took place and I said, "There's a priority."

I saw that my children needed more of my life and more of my time, so I made some changes in my schedule and set some priorities. The church and the family are flourishing very well.

This is an hour when you must make an extra effort to build your family on the power of God and watch with the anointing of the Holy Spirit against the enemy. Even if your children are grown, you still have authority in the realm of the Spirit to pray for them and stand on the Word of God against the works of the enemy in their lives.

28

Framing Your Child
With the Word of God

By faith we understand that the worlds were framed by the word of God, so that the things which are seen were not made of things which are visible.

Hebrews 11:3

Through God's Word and faith in His Word, He framed the worlds. In Genesis 1, one phrase is repeatedly used: *And God said.* Then what He spoke came to pass.

God called things that were not as though they already were (Rom. 4:17), and with children, it's important that we call them blessed. It's important to speak what we desire to see in them based upon God's Word rather than coming into agreement with existing negative circumstances.

A few examples of framing your children with God's Word are:

"All your children shall be taught by the Lord, and great shall be the peace of your children."

Isaiah 54:13

Using this verse, you can frame your children by saying: *"My children are taught of the Lord, and great is the peace of my children."*

And you, fathers, do not provoke your children to wrath, but bring them up in the training and admonition of the Lord.

Ephesians 6:4

Using this verse, you can frame your children by saying: *"My children are raised up in the nurture and admonition of the Lord. Thank God, my children hear the voice of the Holy Spirit."*

"If you are willing and obedient, you shall eat the good of the land."

Isaiah 1:19

You can frame your children by saying: *"My children are willing and obedient, and they eat the good of the land."*

Delight yourself also in the Lord, And He shall give you the desires of your heart.

Psalm 37:4

You can frame your children by saying: *"My children delight themselves in the Lord, and He gives them the desires of their heart."*

As you frame your children with the Word of God, what you speak over them will come to pass, because the Word is . . . **living and powerful, and sharper than any two-edged sword, piercing even to the division of soul and spirit, and of joints and marrow, and is a discerner of the thoughts and intents of the heart** (Heb. 4:12).

A couple who were on staff at Victory Christian Center a few years ago and who are now pastoring, shared how their three boys took turns reading Charles Capps' confession book when they traveled in the car. One would read the confessions, such as: *"I am a new creature in Christ Jesus. Greater is He Who is in me than he who is in the world."* Then everyone else would repeat it. In this way, God's Word of who they are in Christ was instilled in them. Today, these three young men are walking in the light of God's Word, because their parents sowed the Word into their lives.

Each day I frame my children with the Word of God. For example: *"Father, I thank You that Your angels are watching over Sarah, Ruth, John, and Paul, and they are protected day and night. I thank You that they're delivered from all evil. I thank You that the helmet of salvation is about them and the blood of Jesus covers them. I thank You, Lord Jesus, that You are teaching them and working in them, both to will and to do Your good pleasure.''*

The principle of framing your children with the Word of God should also be used over your mate and others. In this way, you're speaking what should be rather than reinforcing negative circumstances.

One example of framing your wife or husband with the word is:

Husbands, love your wives, as Christ loved the church and gave Himself up for her.

Ephesians 5:25 AMP

. . . let each man of you (without exception) love his wife as [being in a sense] his very own self; and let the wife see that she respects and reverences her husband — that she notices him, regards him, honors him, prefers him, venerates and esteems him; and that she defers to him, praises him, and loves and admires him exceedingly.

Ephesians 5:33 AMP

Husband, you can frame your wife with the Word by saying: *"My wife respects and reverences me, notices and regards me, honors and prefers me, and venerates and esteems me. She defers to me, praises, loves, and admires me exceedingly."*

Wife, you can frame your husband with the Word by saying: *"My husband loves me as Christ loves the Church, and he gives himself up for me."*

To frame someone with the Word is to speak what the Word says in spite of contrary circumstances. The Word will prevail if you doubt not in your heart and if you absolutely refuse to speak negatives.

It's not too late to begin today to frame your children, mate and others with the Word of God.

29

Bless Your Children

Then they brought young children to Him [Jesus], that He might touch them; but the disciples rebuked those who brought them.

But when Jesus saw it, He was greatly displeased and said to them, "Let the little children come to Me, and do not forbid them; for of such is the kingdom of God.

"Assuredly, I say to you, whoever does not receive the kingdom of God as a little child will by no means enter it."

And He took them up in His arms, put His hands on them, and blessed them.

Mark 10:13-16

When was the last time you took up a little child in your arms and blessed them in the power of the Holy Spirit? We need to touch our children and bless them just as Jesus took them up in His arms and blessed them.

The disciples said, "Don't bother the Master. Don't trouble Him." But Jesus said, ..."Let the little children come to Me...." Jesus wasn't uptight with little children, and neither should we be uptight with them!

30

Ten Commandments for Parents

These "Ten Commandments for Parents,"[1] if obeyed, will improve your relationships with your children.

1. *Thou shalt start with thyself.* As parents, set the example so your children have something to follow. You can't set rules and regulations and then disobey them yourself.

2. *Thou shalt be more concerned about relationships than rules.* Jesus said that He didn't come to do away with the law, but He came to fulfill the law (Matt. 5:17), so don't do away with the boundaries, rules, and regulations, because they're necessary. But you must give love and build relationships with your children.

3. *Thou shalt impart the faith.* Deuteronomy 6:5-9 talks about how we're to sit down with our children and talk to them about the Word. We're to share the Word with them as we go throughout the house, and we're to write the Word over the door posts of our homes.

"You shall love the Lord your God with all your heart, with all your soul, and with all your might.

"And these words which I command you today shall be in your heart;

"you shall teach them diligently to your children, and shall talk of them when you sit in your house, when you walk by the way, when you lie down, and when you rise up.

---

[1]Michael Davies, "Ten Commandments for Parents," Associated Church Press, American Tract Society, P. O. Box 462008, Garland, TX 75046.

"You shall bind them as a sign on your hand, and they shall be as frontlets between your eyes.

"You shall write them on the doorposts of your house and on your gates."

4. *Thou shalt learn to listen.* Most parents need to work on this one! James 1:19 says, **...let every man be swift to hear, slow to speak, slow to wrath.** It takes effort to listen to children and teenagers, to get down on their level, to be able to relate to them and really listen to what they're saying, but it's very important to them.

5. *Thou shalt spend time with thy children.* God dealt with me when Sarah was a baby that time with my children was not lost time. It was invested time, and it was quality time. I always had the idea that it wasn't really that important. I thought what was important was the ministry, but God began to reorient my priorities to include time with my family.

I had to reorient myself to learn to play with Strawberry Shortcake and Lemon Meringue dolls and make pies and eat whatever Sarah and Ruthie cooked!

Sometimes parents think they're spending time with the children when they go home and turn on the TV set. That's not quality time. Quality time is when you pay individual attention to your children, sharing with them, and listening to them.

If you'll build a relationship with your children when they are small, when they get older, they'll want to have time with you. In other words, if I spend time with them at a young age, riding bikes with the girls, playing games that are on their level, and playing airplanes and trucks with John and Paul right now, I'll be building an eternal relationship which will continually be strengthened.

When I was playing barrettes with my girls, my first thought was, "I've got better things to do." The Lord let me know, "This is where you need to be, with them."

The "macho image" which the world has projected upon men implies that if you're going to be a man, you need to distance yourself from little children and refrain from crying and being tender. God hasn't called us to be like the god of this world. He has called us to be like Jesus Who said, ...**"Let the little children come to Me, and do not forbid them; for of such is the kingdom of heaven"** (Matt. 19:14). Then, ...**He laid His hands on them**... (v. 15).

I help put the children to bed at night. On one particular occasion when I put the boys to bed, John was out like a light, but Paul just lay there. He said, "Daddy."

"Yes, Paul."

"I love you."

"I love you, too, Paul."

Then he said, "Why don't you come in here and love me then?"

I had already hugged him, kissed him, prayed with him, and read the Bible. There was a need in his life to be touched. Every child needs to be touched and ministered to with the love of God. As a parent, you have the power to minister love.

My greatest joy, outside of the Lord and worshipping Him, is my family. I love to be with my family. I love my wife. We're a team. I love my children. If you're going to be a father, you've got to learn to spend time with your children and do what they like to do.

I enjoy spending time with my children. John is learning to play soccer. He really hasn't figured out what it's all about yet, but he likes to run around. He likes the break time when he can get a drink of water! Recently, when he came off the field, his question to me was, "Daddy, did I do good?" What was he really asking? He wanted my approval as a parent. I think about how many children go without that reinforcement and approval in their lives.

How do we save people from getting on drugs and alcohol? If the deepest needs of their life are met, especially when they're small, they won't have these needs. They won't be vulnerable to those things. When basic needs are not met, people often search in every avenue they can. In a study that took place on the West Coast with prostitutes, it was discovered that over 95 percent of them came from families where there was no positive father image. What were they seeking in prostitution? A craving for what they never received at home.

Where there has been a void, there's a greater tendency to become involved in homosexuality. For the greatest percentage of the young boys involved in homosexuality, either there was an absentee father or a father who lacked spiritual fortitude. The sins of the fathers, the Scripture says, will be visited to the third and fourth generation. When there's a breakdown in the family, it doesn't just affect the fathers. It can affect four generations of families. Are you beginning to see the importance of letting the Lord build our marriages and homes?

6. *Thou shalt acknowledge thy faults as a parent.* James 5:16 says, **Confess your trespasses to one another, and pray for one another, that you may be healed....** Be quick to humble yourself and ask forgiveness of your children when you've made a mistake.

7. *Thou shalt keep a sense of humor.* A good laugh will set you free from pent-up emotions. After we discipline our children, we love them and then say, "You'd better put on a happy face." The children can't help but smile, and then we laugh. Sometimes we laugh about things and they don't even know what we're laughing about, but they'll start laughing and then we all get tickled. Laughter is like medicine.

8. *Thou shalt treat thy children equally.* Children are all different, and as parents, we should never compare them.

9. *Thou shalt use discipline.* (We've already discussed this one!)

10. *Thou shalt know when to let go.* Sometimes parents tend to overprotect their children. Sometimes parents feel like they've got to be every place the children are, which is a spirit of fear. There's a point where you have to let go and trust God, believing that the training you've instilled in them will preserve and keep them.

It's so important to pray and intercede for your children. We've had many examples where parents have either seen into the Spirit or were quickened by the Spirit to pray for their children. Because of prayer, the enemy was stopped from destroying or coming against their lives.

31

Improving Communication Skills

Good communication involves talking, listening, understanding, and taking action. The Greek word for *communicate* is *koinonia*, which also means "fellowship" and deals with the relationships we have with each other.

Communication breakdown is the number one problem area in marriage. It's the number one cause of separation and divorce. A lot of people don't realize it, because they relate their problems to some other area. But if your communication is proper and you have an ability to share openly, you can solve financial problems, physical relationship problems, and children problems.

Pride and selfishness are the two root causes of problems with communication. If you'll work on those two areas, you'll solve the majority of the communication problems in your family.

Let no corrupt communication proceed out of your mouth, but what is good for necessary edification, that it may impart grace to the hearers.

Ephesians 4:29

This means, let no bad words, no destructive words, no words that put people down or defeat God's purpose; let no words that would bring animosity or ill will or a bad reputation to someone; let none of those words come out of your mouth, but only that which is good to the use of building up. The key to effective communication is speaking words that build up.

And do not grieve the Holy Spirit of God, by whom you were sealed for the day of redemption.

Ephesians 4:30

This means it's possible to grieve the Spirit of God by speaking words that do not edify. As I read through the four Gospels, I notice that Jesus always encouraged and lifted people above the situations and circumstances that came into their lives. That's the way it should be with us.

Let all bitterness, wrath, anger, clamor, and evil speaking be put away from you, with all malice.

Ephesians 4:31

Malice is the bad attitude of wanting to get back at someone, wanting to put them down.

And be kind to one another, tenderhearted, forgiving one another, just as God in Christ also forgave you.

Ephesians 4:32

One of the greatest keys to keeping communication lines open is *keeping the forgiveness lines open.* Whenever there's a stoppage in forgiveness between two people, and they're not walking in forgiveness, then you can count on a breakdown in the communication lines. But where there is forgiveness flowing both directions, the communication lines will remain open.

The Spirit of God spoke to Jeremiah, saying:

"See, I have this day set you over the nations and over the kingdoms, to root out and to pull down, to destroy and to throw down, to build and to plant."

Jeremiah 1:10

We want to pull down strongholds and tear out the things that are hindrances in our lives so we can build strong relationships in our homes and marriages by having a strong, effective communication system.

If you can get your communication right with God, you can have the right communication with the people around you. This includes your spouse, your children, and the people with whom you work. If you talk to God, listen to Him, and seek to understand His ways, then you can have good communication with people.

What often happens is we let down in one of these areas. We either talk to God but we don't listen to Him, or we talk to Him and we may listen to Him a little bit, but we don't really seek to understand what He's saying. Hebrews 13:16 (KJV) says:

But to do good and to communicate forget not: for with such sacrifices God is well pleased.

It takes an effort on your part to communicate effectively with God and with the people who are around you. Although it takes an effort, and sometimes a sacrifice on your part, God says that with this type of sacrifice He is well pleased.

Communication is a process, and it's either verbal or non-verbal. You can communicate without speaking.

Sharon has a good word on this subject: "Proverbs speaks of the 'strange' woman, which usually refers to the prostitute. (Her ways are often an example of non-verbal communication.) I can be in a crowd, and I'll watch people. I've seen people look at other people, and I know those looks. They don't even have to say anything and you know what they're communicating to the other person. When I see someone look at me in the wrong way, if I look away from them and they're still looking at me, I confront them. I say, 'Brother, I feel like I'm supposed to pray for you. I feel like the devil is trying to come against your life.'

"If you see a woman who's flashing her eyes at you in the wrong way, it's time to confront the devil head on. I'm tired of this stuff in the Body of Christ. I've seen too much of it, and it's time to stop it. Look at them eye to eye and pray in the Spirit. That will usually stop it.

"The root of the problem is that most of the time people like this type of attention because it feeds their ego. Don't give place to the devil in this type of seductive trap.

"Proverbs has a lot to say about staying away from the seductress. Proverbs 7:27 says, **Her house is the way to hell....** That's pretty plain!

"Take pleasure in your mate, and don't let the devil look at you in ways that aren't pleasing to God."

Communication is listening and understanding what the other person is trying to express with accurate empathy. Communication is opening up and sharing yourself with another person, even if it means becoming vulnerable.

Don't avoid relationships just because someone will speak the truth to you. I believe you can speak the truth in love (Eph. 4:15), but you need to learn how to *hear* without being easily offended. Don't wear your feelings on your sleeve!

Communication specialists indicate that when you talk with another person, there are actually six messages that can come through as a result of your communication:

1. What you mean to say.
2. What you actually say.
3. What the other person heard you say.
4. What the other person thinks they heard you say.
5. What the other person says about what you said.
6. What you think the other person said about what you said.

Communication is so important. It's the bridge that brings two different people together. *Frustration usually ends where communication begins.*

32

Seven Keys
To Improving
Your Communication Skills

1. *Make a decision to improve communication.* Just as loving your mate is a decision, not an emotion or a feeling, so you must make a decision that you want to improve your communication skills.

2. *Establish a quality time to share and communicate with your mate and family.* Indicate a time on your calendar for your mate and your children if you're extremely busy. It's more important than all the ball games, sporting events, recreational activities, and all the other things that you'll do.

God dealt with me that I needed to make appointments to meet with Sharon. As husband and wife, you need to make plans concerning your children — their education, vacations — and the time that you will be alone with each other and them in a family setting. When Sharon and I began to pull away together, we were able to eliminate a lot of frustrating situations by planning those things that were important.

We began to share common goals and dreams: What are the goals we have for our family? Where will we be at the end of this year in our lives spiritually? Where do we want to be five years from now?

It's important that your sharing time not be a distressing time. In other words, if you both work downtown and you have just come through the five o'clock rush hour and haven't eaten yet, that's no time to communicate on something you have different opinions about.

What's the principle that businessmen use when they're going to make a deal or talk with someone about a problem? They take them out to lunch or dinner, and after they've eaten and are full and happy, they talk about the situation.

I believe a lot of arguments are started when people are in stress situations. They try to resolve a problem in a few minutes when they only have a short time, or when they're not feeling right. It would be much better just to put it off until there's time to discuss it in a relaxing atmosphere.

TV is probably the greatest enemy of communication. When I was growing up, we used to bow down and worship the god of TV, offering the evening sacrifice of ten eyes for about three hours. After we had worshipped, then the god of television would impart to us his spirit, and we would go to sleep with that spirit. Then the next day, we would go out and walk in the light of that which we had received! How many people follow this pattern today?

3. *Take an interest in what the other person is doing.* The best communicators are the ones who show an interest in the other person. The opposite of this is selfishness. It's not hard to listen to someone if you take an active interest in what they're doing.

Jesus came to our level to lift us to His level. This same principle applies in communication. When you come to the level where people are to communicate with them, you'll be able to move into levels where they can communicate with you and receive what you're saying.

4. *Be willing to admit that you've been wrong.* What's the root problem of not being able to admit that you've been wrong? Pride. Here's an example: "It couldn't possibly have

been my fault! If it was my fault, it was only two percent my fault and 98 percent yours!''

When there's an unwillingness to admit wrong, then there's going to be a communication breakdown. But when there's a willingness to say, ''I made a mistake, I misunderstood, I misinterpreted, I said the wrong thing, I had the wrong attitude,'' healing is released.

James 4:6 says, . . . *"God resists the proud, but gives grace to the humble.''* In family and marriage relationships, when someone refuses to admit wrong, you naturally resist them. There's a wall that's automatically built.

5. *Be willing to accept constructive criticism.* Defensiveness will stop the flow of communication.

6. *Avoid cutting and belittling remarks.* I've heard it said, ''Laughter at the expense of another person is the lowest form of humor.'' The truth is, it's really not humor at all. Husbands and wives destroy their marriages from the inside out when they make ''cute remarks'' that cut or belittle their mate or children. Cute little remarks which cut another person fit into the category of corrupt communication, and it grieves the Holy Spirit.

7. *Be sure that outside obligations aren't robbing you of time with your mate and family.* Civic and community involvements can come between you and your family. Chose activities that can involve each family member.

Sometimes parents will sacrifice their time together to have time with the children, but you not only need to have time individually with the children, you need time alone with one another as husband and wife.

33

Levels of Communication

There are five basic levels of communication. As we discuss these levels, mentally think about the level of conversation you have most of the time with your spouse, your children, your employer, and with God.

1. *Cliche level.* A conversation at this level goes something like this. "Hi, how are you? The weather is fine today, isn't it?"

2. *Factual level.* Conversing on this level of communication is like quoting statistics or reporting the five o'clock news! "I went to work today. I came home. I bought a gallon of milk." A great deal of conversation transpires on this level, particularly among men. Men tend to think in terms of headlines, while women think more in terms of the fine print. They want all the details!

3. *Personal judgment level.* For example, "I think we ought to send our children (or grandchildren) to Christian school." You're expressing your own judgment about something.

If a person feels rejected at this level of communication, many times he'll withdraw and go back up to the second or even the first level.

4. *Emotional/feeling level.* On this level, you begin to express your feelings and emotions. For example, "You were insensitive when you said that to me."

It's important to get to this level of communication. You become vulnerable at this level, particularly if you have a feeling of insecurity. If someone touches your area of insecurity or weakness, then you'll react.

Sometimes we forget that a soft answer turns away wrath. (Prov. 15:1.) This is why it's so important to have a relationship with God and have His Word working in your heart. Then when these situations occur, you won't blow up. (Remember in your communication to attack the problem and not the person.)

5. *Total openness and transparency level.* The goal in marriage and family relationships is to move into this level of communication where you can share completely and freely about anything and everything. At this level, there are no areas that you have to hide or cover up, no areas where you are limited or where you feel there's a touchy subject you can't talk about.

Genesis 2:24,25 relates to total honesty and transparency in communication in marriage:

> **Therefore a man shall leave his father and mother and be joined to his wife, and they shall become one flesh.**
>
> **And they were both naked, the man and his wife, and were not ashamed.**

In other words, there was nothing hidden. In communication, you must have transparency with nothing hidden, an openness with each other to know what the other person is thinking or feeling.

You can avoid challenges in a marriage as you learn how to communicate. Women seem to talk more freely than men, and for this reason, women need to work at being better listeners.

There are reasons why people either won't talk or are hesitant to talk. Sometimes they're afraid people will reject what they have to say, put them down, or embarrass or criticize them. That's the way it is in some relationships. One spouse won't talk, because any time they say something, the other person puts them down with, ''You're so dumb.''

Or they're out in a crowd and their mate makes them the butt of a joke. The man tells a joke about his wife, or the wife tells a joke about her husband. After a while, that person clams up and won't talk. We have to break through these barriers and fears.

Men sometimes have difficulty in putting into words what they really want to say, although women sometimes have a challenge in verbalizing their thoughts, too.

There may have been something in your family while you were growing up that kept you from communicating at the fifth level. Sharon's family communicated on this level of total openness and transparency with one another. We didn't have that same freedom in my home. Since that time, it has been developed in our family members, but I had to learn to break through the fear of communicating what was really on my heart.

34

Communicating on an Intimate Level

As our church began to increase in the early years, I shared more intimately about our dreams and visions among the staff than I did with my wife. I developed a relationship with the men in leadership positions because of the goals and dreams that we shared.

I now realize that this is the case with many businessmen and businesswomen. They talk more intimately of their feelings, desires, plans, and visions with the people at work than they do with their mate.

The time came when I realized I needed to open up and talk to Sharon. She would talk to me about several things and ask me what was going on, and I would say, ''Oh, not much.'' I would just shrug it off or say a few brief words. But I needed to open up and tell her what was deep in my heart.

One of the greatest joys of our relationship today is the deep, heart-to-heart talks on a daily basis. It doesn't take us forever to get to the fifth level of communication. We live on that level.

It takes a willingness to be open and pull off the mask to get to the fifth level of communication and let the person with whom you dwell know exactly where you are, what your goals and dreams are, and to be vulnerable.

When you open yourself up in this way, you are open for criticism. But until you put yourself in this position, you'll never know the depth of intimacy of the relationship God has planned.

I found that as I opened myself up and began to share with my wife, she opened her heart up to me. I'm talking about being married, living together, and ministering together. Our relationship has deepened as we've been open in our communication with each other.

I'll never forget a youth counselor in one of the churches I served as a youth director. I went to see this man and his wife in their home. They showed me through their beautiful house. When they took me into their bedroom, they said, "Each night in this room, we talk to each other and solve all the world's problems together." That struck inside of me. Here was a couple who were happily married with two beautiful children. They had learned to communicate.

You need to set aside a time when you can open up and communicate with your mate on a regular basis, whether it's over coffee in the morning, at breakfast or lunch, in the evening on the back porch or whenever. Identify some place where you can open up and share together freely.

35

Reasons People Aren't Transparent in Communication

One of the first reasons people don't share and communicate openly is the *fear of being ignored.* They fear that someone won't pay attention or listen to their ideas, thoughts, feelings, or what they have to share.

Many times parents build a communication barrier into children by failing to respond to them when they share their innermost secrets. So the child begins to think, "Well, why should I share with my parents? They're not interested. They don't even hear me." No matter how insignificant it may seem, it's important to listen to your children.

Another reason people don't go into deeper levels of communication is the *fear of rejection,* the fear they will be rejected.

Another reason people aren't completely open and transparent in communication is *fear of ridicule.* They are afraid someone will take the things they share and make a mockery of them, belittle them, or twist their words.

If you'll make a positive, conscious effort to rule out ignoring, rejecting, and ridiculing from your relationships, you can improve the communication in your home.

Many ideas have been killed by rejection before they ever got off the ground. Sometimes an idea may sound really crazy and far out, but it's not to be rejected at that moment. Just say, "Well, let's think about it. Let's pray about it. Let's take some time and develop that thought."

It's important in relationships in the home to welcome ideas or thoughts presented, particularly by children. Their ideas should not be thrown out the window, rejected, ridiculed, or belittled.

I have worked with teens most of our ministry. I have found that parents must make an adjustment when their youngsters move into adolescence. Children go through a biological, chemical, and emotional change when they get to be 11, 12, 13 or 14. When they hit that age, if you continue to treat them the way you did when they were younger, there's going to be an automatic communication breakdown and barrier. There has to be an adjustment in the way you relate to the adolescent child, gradually moving them into an adult relationship in communication. This, of course, demands more trust on the part of the parents, utilizing faith in God to a greater dimension.

Sharon's friends used to come over to her home to talk to her mother. They were interested in talking to her, because she had learned the secret of how to relate to teenagers and not treat them as small children.

36

Don't Communicate in Anger

It's good to understand that even though you are open and transparent with one another, you should not communicate in anger. James 1:20 says, **For the wrath of man does not produce the righteousness of God.** If you're going to walk in righteousness (right standing with God), you must learn how to communicate without wrath. One way to maintain self-control is to pray in the Spirit.

Once you've been hurt or offended, if you feel wrath rising up inside, you may need to go in another room and pray in the Spirit. Or you may need to wait overnight before talking about it in order to avoid communicating in wrath. If you let your emotions get carried away, then the other person can't really hear what you're saying. All they hear is anger, but you want them to understand. In order for them to hear, you must be in control of your emotions.

I believe God placed the fruit of the Holy Spirit in our human spirit so it could mature to be able to handle all situations with love, joy, peace, longsuffering, kindness, goodness, faithfulness, gentleness, and self-control. (Gal. 5:22,23.)

The only time Jesus became angry was with righteous indignation as He dealt with the money changers in the temple and with the scribes and Pharisees, but this was the anger of God at religious traditions. There's a big difference between the anger of God and the wrath of man, so we need to discern this in our hearts.

One of the biggest detriments to good communication is allowing the emotions to become involved. An emotional outburst can cause a breakdown in communication. But if you can share without emotional involvement, shouting or getting upset, you can resolve problems in a godly manner.

Ephesians 4:26,27 says:

> *"Be angry, and do not sin"*: **do not let the sun go down on your wrath, nor give place to the devil.**

I believe God gave us the emotion of anger to combat the works of the devil. If we would fight the devil as hard as we fight each other, we would be living in peace and harmony with each other. Many marriages would be better if the husband and wife clearly understood that *they're on the same side!* They're working as a team. Your marriage takes team effort, for a house divided against itself will not stand. (Matt. 12:25). You need to acknowledge that you're a team player alongside your wife or husband. As you flow together, you will succeed. You will reach your goals and be able to claim your victories.

37
Don't Bring Up the Past

In good communication, there's a balance in speaking the truth in love. Truth without love becomes harsh, and love without truth becomes passive and ineffective.

We're not talking about going back and digging up some old thing that's been dead for 25 years and bringing it out to examine it, unless it's a hindrance in the relationship. When you come to the Lord and ask forgiveness, your past is under the blood of Jesus Christ, and in Him there's no condemnation or guilt.

We have had to be very specific about this in marriage counseling, because we've had people who wanted to go back, dig up and review, play by play, something that happened years earlier. That is the devil's tool to use against the relationship.

Before marriage, you should be totally honest with each other in finances, in children from a previous marriage, or in anything that will be pertinent to the relationship if it's found out later. Then after you're married, or when you come to Jesus, your past is under the blood of Jesus.

Don't go back and talk about the girlfriend you had when you were sixteen, the boyfriend at seventeen, or all those past mistakes of your mate. It's like digging up an old dead animal. It's going to smell worse every time you dig it up. Don't do it. It's under the blood of Jesus. Live from this day *forward:*

> ...forgetting those things which are behind and reaching forward to those things which are ahead.
>
> **Philippians 3:13**

If your mate tells you something from the past, then listen, pray, forgive, release, and let go! But be led by the Spirit of God in sharing things that are already under the blood of Jesus.

38

The Power of Agreement in Communication

Strong communication produces an atmosphere in which you can speak the word of faith in agreement. The most powerful force on earth is a husband and wife who are in agreement and united in speaking the word of faith. There's no closer union that can take place.

Jesus said:

> "...if two of you agree on earth concerning anything that they ask, it will be done for them by My Father in heaven.
>
> "For where two or three are gathered together in My name, I am there in the midst of them."
>
> Matthew 18:19,20

So what's the devil after in breaking up communication? He's trying to destroy the greatest power source that God has on the face of the earth and that is the agreement of husband and wife. Now, this doesn't mean that two people, other than husband and wife, can't come together and see great results from the power in their agreement. When I pray with my staff members, there's power in our agreement, for we are in unity in our spirits.

The Lord said that Sharon and I had to come into a place of agreement in our spirits, and we should never let anything break the power of that agreement. Now, we have challenges because we are human. In fact, at times I think we're more human than anyone else! Sometimes people

109

look at leadership and think that people in those positions don't have difficulties, that they don't have tempers they have to deal with or problems to work through. I've got news for you. We've had all of these things. We have to learn to forgive, to ask forgiveness, to show mercy and receive mercy.

We must determine to tear down the things in our marriages and families and in the Body of Christ that would keep us from coming into agreement. Then when you touch and agree for your children, you know the power of God is active. When you speak concerning a situation in the church, you know the power of God is working. If you're a single parent and you come into agreement with your children, you know the power of God is released. Everyone needs someone to agree with them in prayer.

39

Flowing Together
as Husband and Wife

First Peter 3 gives some practical principles on how to flow together as husband and wife. We'll look at a portion of this chapter verse by verse.

> **In like manner you married women, be submissive to your own husbands — subordinate yourselves as being secondary to and dependent on them, and adapt yourselves to them. So that even if any do not obey the Word [of God], they may be won over not by discussion but by the [godly] lives of their wives.**
>
> **1 Peter 3:1 AMP**

This verse says that wives are to *adapt* themselves to their husbands. This does not imply a "doormat" relationship. To *adapt* yourself means to "fit and flow together."

The *New King James Version* of this verse says:

> **Likewise you wives, be *submissive* to your own husbands....**

To be *submissive* also means to "fit and flow together as husband and wife."

The *King James Version* of this verse says:

> **Likewise, ye wives, be in subjection to your own husbands; that, if any obey not the word, they also may without the word be won by the *conversation* of the wives.**

In this translation, *conversation* doesn't mean talking or babbling! To be "won by the *conversation* of the wives" in King James English means to be "won by the godly lifestyle of the wives."

Verse 2 in the *King James Version* goes on:

While they behold your chaste conversation coupled with fear.

This means the husband will see how the wife fears (obeys) God, and he'll see a quality of life, a meekness and a tenderness in her.

Whose adorning let it not be that outward adorning of plaiting the hair, and of wearing of gold, or of putting on of apparel.

1 Peter 3:3 KJV

Many people have interpreted this verse to mean that you're not supposed to wear jewelry or fix your hair. Now, if they're going to interpret the first part of this verse this way, then they need to interpret the last part in a similar manner. They should interpret it, "You're not supposed to put on apparel either!" They all fit together. Obviously, the focus is on moderation.

What is the Spirit of God trying to convey to us? I believe He's saying, "Don't let the outward decoration that you put on, and the improvements that you make outwardly, outdo the inward improvements that you make."

Verse 4 in the *King James Version* says:

But let it be the hidden man of the heart, in that which is not corruptible, even the ornament of a meek and quiet spirit, which is in the sight of God of great price.

In other words, the ornament of God (decoration, jewelry, and adornment) is a meek and quiet spirit. God wants all of us to have a meek and quiet spirit. On the contrary, selfishness wants to dominate, take control, and assert itself.

> **For after this manner in the old time the holy women also, who trusted in God, adorned themselves, being in subjection unto their own husbands:**
>
> **Even as Sarah obeyed Abraham, calling him lord: whose daughters ye are, as long as ye do well, and are not afraid with any amazement.**
>
> **Likewise, ye husbands, dwell with them according to knowledge....**
>
> **1 Peter 3:5-7 KJV**

Men need some knowledge about women to understand their wives. It takes Holy Ghost revelation for me to understand my wife.

Honor Your Mate

> **Likewise, ye husbands, dwell with them according to knowledge, giving *honour* unto the wife, as unto the weaker vessel, and as being heirs together of the grace of life; that your prayers be not hindered.**
>
> **1 Peter 3:7 KJV**

To *honor* someone is to treat them the way you want to be treated. How do you want to be treated? Do you want to be treated like a king? Then treat your mate in the same manner. If you're the king, treat her like a queen. If you're the queen, treat him like a king. That treatment will come back to you.

We need to do things together that are special to one or the other. Sharon likes to go out and eat (just the two of us) in one of those places where you can hardly see what you're eating! I can never get them to turn the lights down at McDonald's or Wendy's! When we were dating, we went to the Tastee Freeze and had a Coke with two straws, but it was special.

The amount of money spent isn't the issue. I'm talking about taking the time to spend with your mate, to care for them and listen to them. That builds strong homes and marriages.

When Sharon and I go out to eat without the children, they want to know why we aren't taking them. We tell them, ''Because we love each other.'' We've heard them tell each other, ''Mama and Daddy are going out because they love each other.''

You see, our marriage relationship sets the tone for our relationship with our children. If we lose our own relationship, we're not going to have any for them. But if we keep our relationship strong, then we can keep our love life toward them strong.

Another thing about treating a person the way you want to be treated is in the realm of forgiveness. Be quick to forgive.

Many couples go through periods of unforgiveness, holding grudges, and keeping score of what the husband or wife did or didn't do. Sometimes people can rattle off their score cards in ten seconds, going through the whole list! But when you cancel the list and say, ''I forgive,'' a bond begins to develop. Forgiveness begins with you being willing to say, ''I was wrong; please forgive me.''

Be of One Mind

Finally, be ye all of one mind....

1 Peter 3:8 KJV

It takes an effort to be of one mind (one in thought), but it's possible. Sharon and I dated for three years before we married (some of that time was apart from each other), and we had an opportunity to develop our knowledge of one another.

We thought we knew each other, but we didn't know each other in the depth that we thought. Because we had made the decision to love each other, then we were willing to get to know each other, even when it meant receiving correction from each other.

We've grown in our communication, and we stay on the fifth level of communication where we talk intimately with each other.

Many people don't have the ability to receive or give correction to each other. In order to give correction, you've got to be able to receive it. Always remember that principle, because too many times people are quick to give correction, but it's hard for them to receive it.

The Bible says to get the log or beam out of your own eye, then you'll be able to see clearly how to get the splinter out of the other person's eye. It won't seem as great to you when you're working on yourself to get rid of wrong attitudes and feelings. When you go to the other person, you'll go to them in meekness and humility if you have something to say to them.

Having Compassion One of Another

. . . having compassion one of another, love as brethren, be pitiful, be courteous.

1 Peter 3:8 KJV

To *be pitiful* means to "be sympathetic with each other." You need to be able to feel what your mate is going through. Then this verse says to be courteous with one another. I appreciate the fact that Sharon is courteous to me.

One time when we were at Disneyland, Sharon and I watched people in the heat of the day when the kids were crying, because they were hot and sweaty. What they were eating was melting all over them. A lot of parents weren't real courteous with each other, nor were they real courteous with their children.

Out of the abundance of the heart the mouth will speak. What's down inside your heart will come out in pressure situations. That's why it's important that you spend time with God on a daily basis. When you spend time with Him, then your time in relationships with other people will be strengthened by the Word. What's inside of you will come out in your attitude, words, and thoughts toward others.

Not Rendering Evil for Evil

Not rendering evil for evil, or railing for railing: but contrariwise blessing....

1 Peter 3:9 KJV

In other words, when someone does you wrong, just bless them and be good to them. Sow a blessing to them.

...knowing that ye are thereunto called, that ye should inherit a blessing.

1 Peter 3:9 KJV

If you'll sow a blessing to someone else, it will come back to you. Whatever you sow, you'll reap. (Gal. 6:7.) This is true in every area of life. Plant a seed of love when your mate is going through a difficult time, or when you're in a situation in which it looks like there's strife. Don't join in the strife with the other person. Sow mercy and love into that situation, and you'll see that person change right before your eyes. You will reap what you've sown. If you sow strife, then you'll get strife from the other person.

Before we react, it's important that we stop and ask ourselves, "How would Jesus act in this situation?" Walk in the self-control of the Holy Spirit that you have inside of you. A lot of people say, "Well, I just don't have control. This is just my nature."

No, it's not your nature! But you have the Spirit of God to help you. When you were born again and engrafted into Christ, you received a new nature. But it's up to you to live out that new nature.

Before you take any action or speak any words, stop and get control of yourself. Then say, "Honey, I love you. Let's pray about this." Make sure that what comes from you are words of life, not words of destruction.

> **For he that will love life, and see good days, let him refrain his tongue from evil, and his lips that they speak no guile.**
>
> **1 Peter 3:10 KJV**

If you want to see good days in your marriage, refrain your tongue from speaking evil and deceit. If we will control our tongue from speaking in a detrimental way toward one another, many marriages can be saved. Stop and get control!

Run From Evil

> **Let him eschew evil....**
>
> **1 Peter 3:11 KJV**

To *eschew evil* means to run from it. Run from evil situations. Run from the very appearance of evil. If you're in a situation that's a temptation to you, whether it's on your job or wherever it might be, listen to your heart and obey your spirit.

Abstain from evil. Flee from the very appearance of evil that would try to pull you away from the good life found in Jesus Christ.

> **...and do good; let him seek peace, and ensue it.**
>
> **1 Peter 3:11 KJV**

Go after the good. Seek peace. It takes an effort in a marriage relationship to seek peace — to be a peacemaker, to be a peace maintainer — but you can do it, for the Peacemaker lives inside of you.

The Lord's Eyes and Ears
Are Open to the Righteous

For the eyes of the Lord are over the righteous, and his ears are open unto their prayers: but the face of the Lord is against them that do evil.

1 Peter 3:12 KJV

When you are walking after God's will and making every effort to obey Him, God is open to hear you. But His face is against you if you're going after evil.

And who is he that will harm you, if ye be followers of that which is good?

1 Peter 3:13 KJV

This means that the devil cannot have any place in your life. He can't harm you, he can't get through to your marriage, and he can't get into your life if you're following after that which is good.

It's really important that you not only love each other, but that you appreciate each other as husband and wife.

40

Becoming One Is a Process

Becoming one in marriage is a process. Sharon and I both had some rough edges when we got married. It took us a while to become one mind and Spirit as well as one flesh.

You become one mind by taking time to communicate with each other. You become one in the Spirit realm by communicating what the Spirit of God is saying to you and by listening to what the Spirit of God is saying to your marriage partner.

People talk about everything else. They talk about sports, the weather, housing, business, and personal circumstances. Why don't families talk about the Word of God, what it means, what it can do, and what's happening with the Word in each of their lives?

It's possible for two people to live together a long time and yet never grow any closer spiritually. They're one flesh as far as the physical aspect, and they may even be one mind in the sense that they're able to talk about hobbies, activities, and common interests. But as far as the Spirit realm, they're no more unified than they were when they first got married.

As a married couple, it should be one of your goals in life to grow closer and stronger in the realm of the Spirit, to the point that you can even pick up in the Spirit what God is speaking to your mate, where they are in the realm of the Spirit, and what Word is needed to encourage them.

41

Appreciating Your Marriage Partner

There's no place in the home for verbal or physical abuse. Berating, belittling, and mocking words spoken to one another depreciate the value of marriage and family relationships.

If you continually depreciate your mate, the day will come when you'll see no value in the marriage relationship. But when you speak positive, affirming, and encouraging words to your mate, you'll appreciate the value of your marriage.

The more you speak well of that one you're married to, the more you have reason to stay married to that person, because the value of your marriage relationship goes up.

Appreciation and depreciation both are linked to the words that come from the lips of the marriage partners. There's a way to solve conflicts and differences without throwing pots and pans, without knocking heads, and without screaming. There's a way to resolve differences with your spirit under control. When your spirit is under control, then when there's an area of improvement needed, you can address it calmly.

42

Men Taking
the Spiritual Leadership
in the Home

When men are in proper relationship to Jesus, they will rise up to be the spiritual leaders in their homes. They will have the spiritual strength they need, and they will have the Word of God to guide them.

Whether the family goes to church or not shouldn't be the wife's decision. It should be the man who says, "We're going to attend church." Men are responsible to set the example of what's important in the family.

Men should set the example in Bible reading in the home. It shouldn't be only at Christmas time that they read the Bible to their family. Thank God that it is done then, but it needs to happen more than once a year. Reading the Word will bring light into the home.

I would like to challenge men to spend as much time reading the Bible in the family as they do reading the newspaper. People often say, "We don't have time." How much time is spent watching television? How much time is spent reading periodicals? How much time is spent reading the newspaper? There's time to read the Bible, but it's a matter of priority.

It's not only the family who prays together who stays together, but it's the family who receives the light of God's Word. Men are responsible, not only for getting the family in church and being the example in the home, but also for prayer in the family.

It's very humbling for men to say, "Let's pray together." It's good for the ego! It's good for men to call the family together and say, "Let's have our devotions together." We have four children and I'll admit, it's an event to get everyone together. Men are responsible for setting the example of what's priority in life.

Most of the problems we're facing in America go back to a default by Christian parents in raising their children in the nurture and admonition of the Lord. When parents don't train their children in the way they should go, in the next generation there's even more secularism and godlessness. We're called to raise a new standard of the Word of God and prayer in our homes.

Men should be the ones to see that goals are established for the family. Businessmen can chart what they're targeting for in the future. Likewise, we should chart that we're targeting to see our children serving God 25 years from now.

43

God Hates Divorce

God hates the sin of divorce. (Mal. 2:16.) Yet God loves those who are divorced. He can redeem and restore.

Marriage is not something that you're just to endure. I believe the only reason a lot of people haven't broken their marriage vows is because of social pressures or concern for their children, but they're living in a cold war, a co-existence together under one roof, and there's no love. They're living in a divorced state under the guise of marriage.

The strongholds over this type of marriage relationship can be torn down in prayer. God can bring you and your mate together in unity and harmony.

In a marriage relationship, unconditional love is a decision. A statement that's often made by a husband to a wife or a wife to a husband is, "I don't love you any more." The love has gone. But if we understand unconditional love, if God's love is in us, then we will decide to let it come out. You can either release it or withhold it. It's not that it's gone, but some haven't allowed it to flow in them.

I often have someone come to me with divorce papers and ask me to pray with them about their situation. I would like to bring healing to those who may be in such a situation, but I would also like to bring prevention for it.

It is the same between a father or mother, children, or teenagers. Perhaps you've said, "I don't love you any more. I want to get out. I want to run." No, you can love, even though there may be circumstances that you're facing at home that aren't right. God's love is not based on what someone is doing to you.

Perhaps you've been mistreated in your home as a teen or as a young person. I have good news for you. You can love your mother and your father or your guardian. You can love them into the Kingdom of God. Unconditional love will break down the barriers.

God hates "putting away" (divorce) for two reasons:

1. *It is a breach of the covenant to which God is a party.* When two people come together in marriage, God is a Third Party to the covenant which they enter. (God actually is the Second Party, because the couple becomes *one flesh.*)

2. *Divorce attacks and affects the godly seed.* Probably the worst thing we see in divorce is what it does to the children.

Malachi 2:14-17 says:

> Yet you say, "For what reason?" Because the Lord has been witness between you and the wife of your youth, with whom you have dealt treacherously; yet she is your companion and your wife by covenant.
>
> But did He not make them one, having a remnant of the Spirit? And why one? He seeks godly offspring. Therefore take heed to your spirit, and let none deal treacherously with the wife of his youth.
>
> "For the Lord God of Israel says that He hates divorce, for it covers one's garment with violence," says the Lord of hosts. "Therefore take heed to your spirit, that you do not deal treacherously."
>
> You have wearied the Lord with your words; yet you say, "In what way have we wearied Him?" In that you say, "Everyone who does evil is good in the sight of the Lord, and He delights in them," or, "Where is the God of justice?"

God is seeking a godly seed: children who will know Him and obey Him.

If you've used the word *divorce* in your home, strike it from your vocabulary, for once you plant that seed in your marriage, it will grow and Satan will make sure it's watered.

One of the reasons we see so much crime and immorality among teenagers and children isn't the fault of the children. It's the fault of the parents. *The children are products of what's taking place in the home.*

When children are raised in a happy home atmosphere, they're able to take a strong stand for Christ as young adults.

When I was dating Sharon, and I went to her home, I had never seen a family that had so much fun together. There was laughter and joy, because Christ was the center of that home. Because of what I saw in her home life, I made a decision that I wanted that kind of family — a family who laughed together without tension.

God has a plan for every family to come to a place of sharing, loving, and ministering to one another in the power of the Spirit of God.

44

The Curse of Divorce
Can Be Broken Off of You

Perhaps you've come from a broken home and the marriage of your parents didn't work out. I want to encourage you: no matter what you've experienced, *you can have a good marriage.* Just because something went wrong in the past in your parents' marriage doesn't mean that wrong has to be passed on in your life.

I have prayed with people who have been divorced, and they were afraid to get married again. In one situation, the man and woman, both in their thirties, had been dating for a length of time. They loved each other, but they were afraid to be joined together because they were fearful of being hurt again.

When young people grow up and have seen a family member go through divorce, there's often a fear in them about getting married. They are afraid of going through the same kind of hurt.

I want to encourage you: the curses that have been upon your life and in your home can be broken off in Jesus' name so you don't have to be afraid if God has called you into a relationship of marriage. You can be free to step into marriage and believe that God can do something wonderful.

45

Issues Causing
Marriage Difficulties

There's such a need in this hour that if we who have strong marriages and homes can catch a vision of being a hospital for hurting marriages, an emergency center, or just a mission station in our neighborhood, our own marriage can go from being good to being a lot better. If your marriage and family are strong in the Lord, you can become a power center of faith to pray and believe God to work in many other homes and marriages.

Although Sharon and I do not condone divorce (we're for "getting it together" in marriage), our church is a place for hurting people, whether they are married, divorced, separated, widowed, or single. Jesus said, "I didn't come for the healthy people, but I came for the sick folks" (paraphrased). This, to us, is what the Gospel is all about. The sick need healing, the broken need mending, and those who are lost need salvation.

If you've gone through a broken marriage, God can reconstruct your life and either use you to help other people as a single or lead you to remarry. God can rebuild your life so you'll avoid making the same mistakes that you've made in the past. It's possible that you can be reconciled to your mate.

I want to address some of the issues that cause difficulties or areas of conflict in the marriage relationship. (We've already briefly touched on some of these issues.)

1. *Pride*. James 4:6 says, . . . *"God resists the proud, but gives grace to the humble."* Proverbs 16:18 says, **Pride goes before destruction, and a haughty spirit before a fall.** A proud person will not receive the grace of God.

Several years ago, I remember going to a home to minister to a couple. The husband was hooked on X-rated movies and the wife was crying out for a healing in their marriage and home. Children were running around in the living room.

I wanted to jerk the guy up by his neck and say, "Don't you see you're losing everything?" He did lose it all. He lost his home, his marriage, and his children. One of the main issues in that man's life was pride. He wanted to do his own thing. It's called the big "I." When you enter marriage, you must be willing to lay down your own ego and take hold of Jesus. We're called not to get, but to give.

We're in a generation now in which many children have grown up in divorced homes. They've gone through tremendous hurts. If they don't receive the ministry of the Holy Ghost, they'll enter a marriage relationship with past scars and wounds.

This is an hour for the Church to rise up as never before because of the number of people who are entering marriage from a totally different perspective. We're in a materialistic, selfish generation. When you get two selfish people together, you have war. They want to grab, they want to get, and they want their own way. In fact, they demand it.

Not one of us is exempt from pride or demanding our own way in certain areas of life. We need to pray, "Lord, I humble myself." To compromise God's Word is wrong, but there's a time when a marriage partner must give in to the other individual. In a family relationship, compromise demands that you give a little, the other person gives a little, and you find a place of common ground.

In many situations today, people demand *all* of what they want. They don't want to give an inch. It's better to have harmony and peace than it is to get your own way, because where there's strife and envy, there's confusion and every evil work. James 3:16 puts it this way: **For where envy and self-seeking exist, confusion and every evil thing will be there.**

This means that even if you get your own way through fighting and demanding, you'll lose ground. You'll lose peace and harmony.

2. *Unforgiveness.* Unforgiveness can cause great difficulty in marriages and families, and it's really tied in with pride.

In Mark 11:25 the Lord says, **"And whenever you stand praying, if you have anything against anyone, forgive him, that your Father in heaven may also forgive you your trespasses."**

Isn't it wonderful that we can be forgiven? **". . . though your sins are like scarlet, they shall be as white as snow; though they are red like crimson, they shall be as wool"** (Is. 1:18).

Some couples keep score and they can do an instant replay on things that have happened over the last 25 years. Sometimes in a marriage, the husband hits the hurt button that charges his wife, or the wife hits the anger button that charges her husband, and suddenly, the replay is on!

A forgiver is a forgetter. A person who says, "I can forgive, but I sure can't forget" has not forgiven, for forgiveness and forgetting are one and the same. When God says, "I will forgive you," He is saying that He will remember your sins no more. (Heb. 8:12.)

Forgetting is an act of your will. Hebrews 12:1 says, **Therefore we also, since we are surrounded by so great a cloud of witnesses, let us lay aside every weight, and the**

sin which so easily ensnares us, and let us run with endurance the race that is set before us.

We must lay aside every weight and sin that would hinder us from running the race God has set before us. Unforgiveness is a horrible burden to bear. We need to cut all the cords of anything that's ever been done to us or against us.

If you have been divorced and you're still harboring some hurts, the power of God will enable you to forgive the offenses of your mate and release them once and for all. If you've already forgiven and forgotten, don't dig anything up. If there are cords of the past that need to be cut, you can cut them by forgiving and releasing the person right now.

In Mark 11:26 Jesus says, **"But if you do not forgive, neither will your Father in heaven forgive your trespasses."** As you forgive the other person, you'll be forgiven.

Sharon and I periodically hold divorce workshops in which we minister to the divorced person as well as to the children who have been involved in a divorced family situation. We can redeem their lives. They don't have to be scarred and wounded. God can put their lives back together.

In our divorce workshops, we deal with the issue of forgiveness, because if you've broken a relationship and violated a covenant, you need forgiveness from God. A lot of people say, "Well, I didn't do anything wrong; it was the other person." We're going to have to go back to step one like the coach with the football team that got beat 50 points in the middle of the season. He walks in the next day and says, "Boys, we're going to start over from the beginning!" He holds up a football and says, "This is a football!"

If you were only two percent wrong, you still need to repent. You need to have a humble heart and ask God's forgiveness so you can start over. You can't carry that old junk into a new relationship and expect it to work. You need to be cleansed from it.

3. *Unmatured fruit.* One of the problems in marriage and family difficulties is that we've majored on everything but the fruit of the Spirit. You can go to any junior college or university and get a degree, but where can you go and get a degree in the joy of the Lord? The peace of God? The love, longsuffering, kindness, goodness, faithfulness, gentleness, and self-control?

Which degree will bring you the most lasting results in life? No one but you can hinder the development of the fruit of the Holy Spirit in your life. Focus your faith and efforts to grow in the fruit of the Spirit.

If there's someone who is joyful in the home, it'll bring healing. Someone who is longsuffering and has the peace of God in a relationship will bring healing to marriage difficulties. Can you imagine a family where the husband, wife, and children are all walking in the love of God? They have the fruit of love. We can go through a lot of techniques and a lot of things we need to do, but we always get back to plain old home cooking! If we'll just get back to the fruit of the Spirit, marriages will work.

So how do we go about developing the fruit of the Spirit? Galatians 5:19-21 gives a list of the works of the flesh: adultery, fornication, uncleanness, licentiousness, idolatry, sorcery, hatred, contentions, jealousies, outbursts of wrath, selfish ambitions, dissensions, heresies, envy, murders, drunkenness, revelries, and the like.

We have to mortify the works of the flesh so that we can develop the fruit of the Spirit. For example, if you've got an angry attitude, don't blame your Irish heritage. Don't blame it on your ancestry. Call it what it is: flesh. It needs to be crucified. That means, "put to death."

When you start to get angry, say "no." When you start to walk in a manifestation of the flesh, cut it off. Stop it at that moment and determine to let the Christ in you, the fruit of the Spirit, rise up through you. Make a decision: *"I will be a love person. I will be a joyful person. I will feed my inner man with the Word of God. I will put God first in my life."*

Do you know that a marriage and home can get sweeter as the years go by? How? The fruit gets better. Hallelujah! The fruit gets sweeter! The longer you live with Jesus, the more you develop the fruit of the Spirit. A marriage that's conceived in God and which allows the fruit of the Spirit to mature will be richer in its latter days than in its first days.

4. *Spiritual maturity.* Spiritual maturity really goes hand in hand with allowing the fruit of the Holy Spirit to mature in the human spirit. In your marriage relationship, if one of you has more spiritual depth and maturity than the other, don't become so superspiritual that you hinder the growth of your mate. Encourage them, speak words of faith to them, and frame them with the Word of God.

Many times husbands draw back into a shell because the wife becomes outspoken concerning the things of the Spirit of God. It's God's desire that you minister to your mate and love them on their level. This may require you to go to ball games or fellowship with them where they are, but if you don't reject them, shove them out, and make them feel put down and less than you, they'll come alongside spiritually.

5. *Jealousy.* Jealousy is another area of conflict in marriage. Proverbs 14:30 (AMP) says, **A calm and undisturbed mind and heart are the life and health of the body, but envy, jealousy, and wrath are as rottenness to the bones.**

Don't give place to jealousy in your life. Jealousy is a result of insecurity. If you have had jealous feelings about your mate or anyone else, ask God to remove the feelings from your life. Ask Him to heal you. Go to the Word of God and find all the scriptures on that area and begin to confess them over yourself: *"I am not jealous. I am secure in You, Lord Jesus. I walk in the love of God."*

On the other side of the coin, don't present situations that would cause jealousy in your mate. Don't allow yourself to be caught in a bad situation with a person of the opposite sex, which would breed jealousy in your mate.

Sometimes a mate becomes jealous when the other person spends too much time at the office or on the job. Be sensitive in your spirit to the needs of your mate, and do your best to fulfill those needs.

6. *Criticizing your mate in front of family and relatives.* When you tell your mother and father negative things about your mate, they'll never forget. Later on in life, when you go through a difficult time in your marriage, your family will remember the negative things you spoke against your partner. They'll bring them to your attention: "Remember, he did this and she didn't do that!"

7. *Criticizing your mate in public.* Another area of conflict is criticizing a mate in public. That's one of the most destructive things that can happen in a marriage, whether it's an open attack or subtle sarcasm.

One couple became so serious about this that in their wedding vows, they promised, "We'll never speak sarcastically about each other in our entire married life."

That's a tremendous commitment to make — never to put down or cut down. Everyone else may be laughing about your mate because of a real cute word that you said, but inside, you're destroying your relationship. You're destroying your intimacy. God tells us to speak words that edify and build up.

8. *Nagging.* Proverbs 27:15 says, **A continual dripping on a very rainy day and a contentious woman are alike.**

This is referring to nagging. Women tend to nag more than men, but men are quite capable of nagging, too.

Sharon used to nag me about my driving! When I would change lanes or pull from a side road onto a main road, she would do one of two things (and sometimes both!). She would gasp, or she would put her hand on the dashboard and press her foot against her side of the car as if she had a brake over there! This began to bug me.

Finally, after I told her she was sucking all the air out of the car, she began to quietly pray. When she left off all those gestures, it had a calming effect on me, and my driving improved! I was causing the problem and needed to change.

If you present yourself in a peaceful way, God will take care of you, but nagging will get you nowhere.

9. *Being ''long'' on words.* Proverbs 10:19 says, **In the multitude of words sin is not lacking, but he who restrains his lips is wise.** In other words, with a multitude of words is sin.

It's important to pray before you confront your mate about something. You need to pray in the Spirit, asking that the Lord will help you come across with a positive, loving attitude. Too many times, people who are honest and frank, but who don't pray before they confront, stir up more strife.

It's like the pendulum that swings two ways. On one side the person will never open up and be honest enough to say anything to the other partner, and on the other side the person is totally honest, open, and frank about everything. However, they stir up strife because they don't know how to walk in a balance and share at the right time. There's a time to share, and there's a way to share.

Ecclesiastes 3:7 says there is **. . . a time to keep silence, and a time to speak.** You need to pray, ''Father, if You want me to speak this to my mate, I ask for You to guide me in speaking it at the right time and in the right way.'' Then it'll come across in a beautiful and edifying way. Your motive should be to edify one another rather than pull each other down.

10. *Don't try to be your mate's Holy Spirit!* Don't try to squeeze your mate into the mold of what you think he (or she) should be. The Holy Spirit is well able to do that.

Romans 12:2 in the J. B. Phillips translation says, **Don't let the world around you squeeze you into its own mould, but let God re-make you so that your whole attitude of mind is changed. Thus you will prove in practice that the will of God's good, acceptable to him and perfect.**

11. *Demonic spirits have been released against marriages.* I don't think most people are aware of the demonic spirits that have been released against marriages. Many people don't know how to pray with authority or how to resist the devil. After you've humbled yourself in the sight of the Lord and submitted yourself to God, you are to ...**Resist the devil and he will flee from you** (James 4:7).

The devil attacks and destroys marriages and some people end up saying, "I don't know what happened." The demonic spirits that are attacking marriages must be dealt with in prayer.

We must know the authority of the believer, how to pray in the Spirit, how to appropriate the promises of God by faith, how to stand and resist the devil with the shield of faith, and how to use the sword of the Spirit (the Word) — for we are in a war. *You must fight for everything that has meaning to you.*

Some people act as though they're in a daze, like the guy I told you about who didn't know he was losing it all. He didn't know the devil had come in and camped in his home. It's as though he was trapped, paralyzed, and mesmerized.

You have to put your foot down: *"In Jesus' name, the devil will not have my family, my home and marriage, or my future home, or the home and marriage of my parents."*

46

Reconciling Differences

Differences need to be reconciled between husbands and wives, mothers and daughters, fathers and sons, and between any two people who have entered into contention. The principles we'll share will certainly not be limited to couples, but will affect your life whether you're married, single, divorced, or widowed.

Have you ever had a difference with a member of your family? Sharon and I have had differences. Sometimes married couples give the impression that they never have problems. Every home faces situations that need to be worked out.

The good news is that there is a solution. There's a way to resolve things peaceably without bloodshed! There's a way to settle an issue besides the divorce court. There's a way to resolve a conflict besides a teenager leaving home.

What is the key to finding God's solutions?

Pride — Open Door to Contention

Proverbs 13:10 says, **By** *pride* **comes only** *contention,* **but with the well-advised is wisdom.** *The Amplified Bible* version says, **By pride and insolence comes only contention, but with the well-advised is skillful and godly Wisdom.**

Pride means "presumption." The idea is that one presumes to have all knowledge and understanding and doesn't need any help or advice. Therefore, when the Bible says, **By pride comes only contention....,** it means that one who is proud produces strife, because he's not open to any other input, particularly anything that differs from his opinion. As a result, he feels that he can never be wrong in his attitude and he produces strife.

The *well-advised* means the "humble person." The humble person is not only open to receive from others, but even more importantly, he's open to receive from God. Now, this should give you a clue as to why the Bible says, **Pride goes before destruction...** (Prov. 16:18). When a person is proud, he will not receive the wisdom of God, and without the wisdom of God, destruction is inevitable.

God resists the proud because the proud are resisting Him. The proud have said, "I have all the answers. I know the way. I don't need God." **By pride comes only contention....** When we submit ourselves and stay open to those around us, then we acknowledge that maybe someone else has a better idea.

Contention leaves when we humble ourselves. The key to removing strife and contention is to walk in humility.

You may be asking, "Well, where did all this pride get started?" It started with Lucifer when he became proud in his heart. He was an archangel of God, the covering anointed cherub. The pride in his heart is revealed in Isaiah 14:12-14:

> **"How you are fallen from heaven, O Lucifer, son of the morning! How you are cut down to the ground, you who weakened the nations!**
>
> **"For you have said in your heart: 'I will ascend into heaven, I will exalt my throne above the stars of God; I will also sit on the mount of the congregation on the farthest sides of the north;**
>
> **'I will ascend above the heights of the clouds, I will be like the Most High.'"**

Ezekiel 28 and 38 also describe Lucifer's position of power. Lucifer lifted up his own heart in pride. The book of Revelation tells us that he led one-third of the angels in rebellion against God.

Because of his prideful position and because of what he had done, Lucifer was condemned and cast out of heaven. Did you know that angels don't have an opportunity to repent? One act of disobedience and they're gone. When there was disobedience, they were cast out.

There was an act of rebellion with Adam and Eve. They got into trouble because of pride:

> **Now the serpent was more cunning than any beast of the field which the Lord God had made. And he said to the woman, "Has God indeed said, 'You shall not eat of every tree of the garden'?"**
>
> **And the woman said to the serpent, "We may eat the fruit of the trees of the garden;**
>
> **"but of the fruit of the tree which is in the midst of the garden, God has said, 'You shall not eat it, nor shall you touch it, lest you die.' "**
>
> **And the serpent said to the woman, "You will not surely die.**
>
> **"For God knows that in the day you eat of it your eyes will be opened, and *you will be like God,* knowing good and evil."**
>
> **Genesis 3:1-5**

Adam and Eve elevated their belief about themselves above what God had told them. They believed they had wisdom and that their opinions and decisions were more important than God's. So they exalted themselves, rebelled, and ate of the forbidden fruit of the tree of the knowledge of good and evil. In that very moment, eternal life went out of them. They lost their righteous position before God, they were separated from the Father, and the fall of the human race took place. They would now give birth to spiritually dead children.

This is why Jesus spoke to Nicodemus, **"...unless one is born again, he cannot see the kingdom of God"** (John 3:3). In other words, every human being on the face of the earth is spiritually dead until he meets Jesus Christ as Lord and Savior. Though a person is physically alive, he is spiritually dead until the Holy Spirit comes in and imparts new life into him.

If you aren't born again, there's a difference between you and God that needs to be reconciled. It can be reconciled in the same way we reconcile differences between other people. That is, if you will humble yourself, God will give you grace.

Some people think they received all the grace they needed 20 years ago. I need grace every day. I live on grace. I run on grace. It's like gas in my tank! I need a continual flow of God's grace in my engine.

Since God gives more grace, He has something to say about how to get grace. The Holy Spirit through James says, ...**"God resists the proud, but gives grace to the humble"** (James 4:6). Grace is God's favor. Grace is God's mercy. Grace is what we've called "the unmerited and unearned favor of God." Grace is God's ability. Another way to define grace is, "God giving us the desire to do His will."

You know, it took a work of grace for some people to want to get saved. You probably didn't even want to. Where did you get the "want to"? It was grace. God imparted, created, and birthed that desire within you. Then once you had the desire, you didn't have the power, so you needed more grace. You needed the ability. God gives us the desire to do His will; then He gives us the ability to do His will. That's the grace of God. He imparts grace to those who will welcome and receive it.

In a family or marriage relationship, contention will come when there is pride and self-exaltation. In other words:

"I want it my way. I want it now. I want it the way I decree it."

So what's the way of reconciliation? "You'd better straighten up!" No! Reconciliation doesn't come by making demands upon someone else. *Reconciliation begins by making a demand upon your own heart.* When you humble yourself, God will give you grace. Maybe it's in the little three-word phrase, "I was wrong."

I'll give you an example. Our little puppy chewed a hole in the screen on our back door. I went out and spanked the puppy and put his nose up to it. I wanted the puppy to get the idea that his behavior was not acceptable! We had four more screens he could reach.

About ten o'clock at night when we were going to bed, our son John crawled in between Sharon and me and out of the clear blue he said, "Daddy?"

"Yes, John."

"You remember when you spanked the puppy?"

"Yes."

"You didn't tell him that you loved him."

John is lying in bed, and the Holy Ghost is talking to him. He realizes that Daddy has messed up, because when John, Paul, Sarah, or Ruthie are disciplined, Daddy and Mama always love them afterwards.

I said, "John, you're right."

I was thinking, "It's 32 degrees outside, and I've got to go out and hug a dog!"

"Okay, John, I'm going."

I went out and said, "Puppy, I forgive you. I love you." I got back in bed, and John was peaceful.

If you humble yourself, God will give you grace to hug a dog! The situation could be with your husband or wife rather than with a puppy, but the principle is the same.

47

Close the Door to Strife

There are times when people have differences of opinion. There's nothing wrong with that. Have you noticed that you and your husband or wife don't always have the same viewpoint? I've noticed that in our marriage! Sharon and I have had to learn how to settle issues when we have different opinions.

Whenever there's a conflict, a difference, or a misunderstanding, that is an open door for strife. Not every difference is strife. Sometimes people get all hung up and say, ''We should never differ on anything if we're really in love.''

You're different and you're married to someone who is different. You may be one who cleans up in the bathroom, and you may have married someone who splashes water everywhere! You may like to get up at the crack of dawn, and you're married to someone who likes to sleep late. It's amazing how God sometimes puts opposites together. You have to learn to work with those differences, appreciate the differences, and flow with them.

You may have children who are opposites. One is really neat, while the other one is really messy. One is always on time, while the other one is always late. One likes things, while the other one likes people.

You have to deal with different people who have different approaches to life. But if a difference or a conflict isn't dealt with properly and brought to an understanding, then it's an open door for strife.

Who is a wise man and endued with knowledge among you? let him shew out of a good conversation [lifestyle] his works with meekness of wisdom.

But if ye have bitter envying and strife in your hearts, glory not, and lie not against the truth.

This wisdom descendeth not from above, but is earthly, sensual, devilish.

For where envying and strife is, there is confusion and every evil work.

But the wisdom that is from above is first pure, then peaceable, gentle, and easy to be entreated, full of mercy and good fruits, without partiality, and without hypocrisy.

And the fruit of righteousness is sown in peace of them that make peace.

James 3:13-18 KJV

James says there are two types of wisdom: 1) wisdom from above, and 2) wisdom from below. The results of envy and strife are confusion and every evil work.

Strife opens the door to calamities, tragedies, accidents, sickness, all types of misunderstandings, bitterness, and imaginations. Strife opens the door to demonic involvement. You'll often find that where there has been demonic involvement in a person's life, there has been strife.

Strife is something you can't afford to play with, because it will tear down the hedge of protection around your home.

God's wisdom (that which is from above) is ... **first pure, then peaceable, gentle, willing to yield, full of mercy and good fruits, without partiality, and without hypocrisy** (James 3:17).

How can you tell if someone has heard from God? Is his message pure? There will never be anything that comes from God that has an atmosphere of immorality, dishonesty, or a lack of integrity. In other words, it's not going to come to create strife. It's going to bring peace. It'll be gentle. It'll be willing to yield. It'll be open to reconsideration and to the input of others. It won't demand its own way. It'll be full of mercy and good fruit. It'll be without partiality. It won't show preference, and it won't be hypocritical or insincere.

James also says, **Now the fruit of righteousness is sown in peace by those who make peace** (James 3:18). The wisdom from God will produce the fruit of love, joy, peace, longsuffering, kindness, goodness, faithfulness, gentleness, and self-control. (Gal. 5:22,23.)

Isaiah 32:17 also says, **The work of righteousness will be peace, and the effect of righteousness, quietness and assurance forever.**

When people are walking in the wisdom of God and ministering His wisdom in their home, there's a righteousness (a right relatedness to God), and the effect of righteousness is quietness and peace in the home. There will be an assurance in the home. This means there will be a security for the children and for the marriage partners.

By the Spirit of God, you can put an end to fights, fusses, and feuds.

"You mean Christians fight, fuss and feud?"

Yes, and we need help in this area.

Make the decision, *"I'm not going to allow strife in my life and in my home."* It begins first of all with you individually.

In 1974 when Sharon and I got hold of the message of faith, we decided we weren't going to allow strife in our marriage and home. So when strife raised its ugly head, it took humility on the part of both of us to quickly go to each other and say, "Whatever I said a while ago, I'm sorry." We stopped strife. We didn't allow it to stay in our marriage relationship. The Bible says, "Be quick to forgive."

Don't give place to the devil. Once you give him a little foothold, he'll take lots more territory if you allow it.

Just because someone else is in strife in the home doesn't mean you have to pitch wood onto the fire! You can walk in peace even when there's strife around you. Jesus Christ left us an example, and if there was ever anyone who walked in the midst of strife, He did. Everywhere He went, people were stirred up and angry at Him, speaking things against Him every time He preached. People were always taking notes and trying to pick at His message and twist His words. Yet, He walked in peace and harmony in the midst of the people of His day.

God can enable us, even in our lives, to walk in peace where there may be strife, but it takes a decision of your will: *"I will not allow strife in my life."*

Does that mean there will never be an opportunity to be angry or to be upset with someone? No. It just means that when the opportunity comes, instead of giving place to it, if you've made a decision with your will, the Holy Spirit will bring that decision to your remembrance and you'll have an opportunity to say, "No, I'm not going to get into strife."

God will move in line with your will. If you will to do something, the Holy Ghost will give you the grace to carry out your decision. Instead of choosing strife, you'll say, "No, I choose to love and forgive."

48

Keys To Giving Strife No Entrance

Can two walk together, unless they are agreed?

Amos 3:3

It's very important that you be in agreement and keep strife out of your marriage and home at all costs, because it's like a cancer. If you allow it to stay and block communication with one another, it will destroy you and your marriage.

Proverbs 25:28 says, **Whoever has no rule over his own spirit is like a city broken down, without walls.** And Proverbs 16:32 says: **He who is slow to anger is better than the mighty, and he who rules his spirit than he who takes a city.** You may be mighty in a lot of ways, but if you don't have control of your spirit, you're not mighty at all. God says the mighty man or woman of God has control over his or her spirit.

Whenever there's a difference, a miscommunication, or a misunderstanding, *deal with it immediately.* Instead of confronting and dealing with a situation, many Christian people say, ''Oh, I'll just let that go.''

If you can let it go, forgive, and get it completely out of your heart and mind, that's one thing. But just to sweep it under the carpet and still have it down in your heart and in your mind is another thing.

If there's a difference, go to the other person. Even if you've forgiven the one involved, if you've not resolved the conflict and difference, there's often a hesitancy to enter into open and honest communion with that individual.

There's a reservation if there's been something in the past that's not been resolved.

When Sharon came to eat with my family while we were dating, I always ate a green salad with my meal. When we got married, she just assumed that I had a salad with every meal. However, the primary time we had it was when we had guests at our house. So the first seven months we were married, it seemed like every time I sat down to eat, whether it was breakfast, lunch, or the evening meal, I was looking at a bowl of green salad!

Now, I like good healthy food so I ate it. Every day! But I kept wondering, "Why are we always having this?" Because I ate it, Sharon thought, "Oh, I'm doing so good, because this is what his mother fed him."

Do you know whose problem it was? It was mine, because I didn't communicate. I can remember the day I came to my last bowl of lettuce! She put it down in front of me, and I was about to cry. I wasn't angry, but she looked at me and asked, "What's wrong?" I said, "Honey, I just can't eat it."

I felt like I did when my daddy made me eat all of the carrots out of my vegetable soup that I'd raked under the bowl! He found them all! I can still remember that night!

Another key to resolving differences and conflicts is *being absolutely honest with other people.* Why are there fewer arguments before marriage than after marriage? Charles Swindoll says it's because before marriage everything you do for each other is voluntary, but after marriage, it's compulsory!

There's a different attitude when you feel you have to do something. So what one person did voluntarily and joyfully before marriage might create a problem later. It's very important that we be open and share. If you don't like doing something or you don't like something about an individual, you're actually being dishonest if you make out like everything is okay. Most people would rather for you to be honest and get it out on the table than to carry resentment and bitterness down on the inside.

Hebrews 12:14,15 says:

Pursue peace with all men, and holiness, without which no one will see the Lord:

looking diligently lest anyone fall short of the grace of God; lest any root of bitterness springing up cause trouble, and by this many become defiled.

Another key to resolving conflicts is to *respond with a soft answer.* **A soft answer turns away wrath, but a harsh word stirs up anger** (Prov. 15:1). When you speak a soft word to people, it soothes and calms. The word *soft* means "gentle and tender." There's a healing balm when you speak a word that's soft to people in the face of a strife-filled reaction to a situation.

In a marriage relationship, or in dealing with children, a soft answer will turn away anger, but when a person's voice begins to escalate, the other person's voice also escalates. It continues to go up until there's a full-scale war. You need to de-escalate these situations by speaking softer and softer until the other person's voice gets softer and softer. In this way, you'll communicate and resolve issues.

49

Tearing Down the Barriers

Love one another with brotherly affection — *as members of one family* — giving precedence and showing honor to one another.

Romans 12:10 AMP

The most powerful force on the earth is the love of God. It was the love of God that sent Jesus to the earth. It was God's love that sent Jesus to the cross. It was God's love that raised Him from the dead.

If we'll learn how to love in the family of God (the Body of Christ), we'll know how to love in our immediate family. The difficulty, however, is that we haven't, in many cases, learned either.

God has called us to minister love. Love will break down barriers that nothing else can break. Sometimes people feel like breaking things over their wife or husband's head to get a message through to them! Now, there's a message that always comes through in that!

Some people feel that by fighting in the family they can resolve differences, but real changes are made *only when we minister love.* Love will penetrate through to someone who has been hardened or mistreated, who has had a difficult background, or who has rejected our love.

What do we usually want to do when we see someone who's angry or bitter, or who strikes out at us? Usually, if we're operating in the flesh, we want to strike back. If we're operating in fear, we want to hit the trail. I mean, we'll let them have it and go. But what does it take to minister love? It takes God's love in us. You can only give what you have.

Some people received the love of God from their parents while they were growing up, while others were deprived of this type of parental love.

If you'll accept Jesus Christ and let His love come into you in its fullness, it will drive out all of the hurt, anger, bitterness, and the sense of being deprived of love from Mom and Dad.

Agape love is the kind of love that Jesus expressed on the cross. I want more of it every day in my life. I need it. God is in me and what I'm really saying is, *"I want to let more of His love flow out of me."* I want to demonstrate it. The Scripture admonishes us, "Walk in love. Put on love."

Technically, theologically, and legally we who are born again have the love of God in us, but in actuality and practice, we have to put it on. We have to release it. We have to activate it so that it will come out — and that comes by a decision.

There may be people you'll have to love on purpose. In other words, it won't come natural. They're not going to draw on your love because of their attitude. You'll have to love them in spite of the way they are!

Usually, when someone is unkind, it's an indication that they're hurting inside. Love recognizes this fact and reaches out to minister to these people to set them free and release them in that area.

I am asking the Father in Jesus' name to let the ministry of love begin to flow through you, whether it's to your family, on the job, to a neighbor who has been indifferent to the Gospel, to an employee who has acted cold and aloof, or to someone you encounter in your daily routine of life.

"I'm asking You, Father, for the anointing of Your Spirit to help us love people through to salvation and to love them through to the healing of their hurts."

Stop what you're doing right now and draw on the love of God!

"Lord, we know it's the Holy Spirit Who sheds Your love abroad in our hearts, so we thank You for pouring it in us and through us. By an act of our will, we will love. We will walk in Your love."

Perfect love casts out fear. (1 John 4:18.) This is the key to winning the lost to Christ.

Our Bible Fellowship pastors, Jerry and Lynn Popenhagen, knocked on the door of a young couple's apartment and loved them out of 29 straight weeks of cocaine addiction. Love drove it out.

Mary Walters, a woman in our church who had been terrified to speak to anyone about Christ, allowed the love of Jesus Christ to do a work in her own heart. She learned how to take the love of God and put it into people.

In one of our tent crusade services, she was sitting beside a woman who said, "I'm an agnostic." My first thought was to cast the devil out of her. (There's a time for that, but this woman needed the devil *loved out of her!* He'll go out either way. You turn the light on and darkness has to flee! You can turn the light on in a number of ways.)

Mary turned the love of God up on the lady who called herself an agnostic by holding her as I prayed over her and spoke the Word of God into her. The agnostic had come because God drew her. She wanted His love, but she had a lot of hurts in her life. Mary just put her arms around her and began to weep in the Spirit. In that prayer and in that ministry of love, the walls in the agnostic's life came down. The hardness, the anger, and the bitterness left.

The miracle of Moses casting the tree into the bitter waters (Ex. 15:22-25) is no greater than the miracle we saw in this woman. When the cross (the tree of Jesus Christ) was cast into the bitter waters of this woman's life, suddenly her twisted face changed into the sweetest countenance I've ever seen. Love did a mighty work in her life.

This same type of love will tear down all the barriers in your marriage, in your family, and in other relationships.

The Spirit of God is destroying the dividing walls that have separated you in your relationships, and it's by the anointing of the Holy Spirit that those imaginations and traditions, those things that have been inherited in your attitudes from your families, are being broken in the name of Jesus. Those things that have separated you from your children, from a relationship of love and unity, by the authority of the name of Jesus, I speak to them that they come down now.

50

Building Your Marriage and Family Upon the Rock

Unless the Lord builds the house,
They labor in vain who build it;
Unless the Lord guards the city,
The watchman stays awake in vain.

Psalm 127:1

You could read this verse, "Unless the Lord builds the *marriage*, they labor in vain who build it." Or "Unless the Lord builds the *family*, they labor in vain who build it."

In other words, even if a watchman arises and sees the enemy coming and knows how to resist him, unless the Lord is guarding that city, it will still be taken.

So it is with the family. Unless the Lord builds and works in our families and in our lives, all the effort we make in the natural will not avail. We must have the power of God in this hour in our homes, marriages, and families.

The family is under attack, and there are no age restrictions. Marriages of 30 and 40 years are disintegrating, because they've never been built by the Lord, or because people have quit allowing the Lord to work in their lives.

When Sharon and I were engaged, the Lord dealt with me that if we didn't build our lives personally upon the right spiritual foundation, as the storms of life came, we would encounter difficulties we were not prepared to handle and our marriage would be blown apart. He didn't say it was a possibility. He said, "It will be."

Jesus said that the winds, the storms, and the rains will beat both upon the house built on the rock and upon the house built on the sand. This isn't a prophetic word. It's simply a statement of fact. The storms will come against your life, your marriage, and your family.

Here's what Jesus said about building upon the Rock:

"Therefore whoever hears these sayings of Mine, and does them, I will liken him to a wise man who built his house on the rock:

"and the rain descended, the floods came, and the winds blew and beat on that house; and it did not fall, for it was founded on the rock.

"Now everyone who hears these sayings of Mine, and does not do them, will be like a foolish man who built his house on the sand:

"and the rain descended, the floods came, and the winds blew and beat on that house; and it fell. And great was its fall."

Matthew 7:24-27

God ordained the marriage union and the family. It was His idea in the beginning. God ordained the marriage to be beautiful and, through it, His plan is to demonstrate His power to the world.

The family is not just a place where people run to hide from the world. Thank God there's strength in the home. God set the family in the community to be a beacon light of salvation and deliverance in the world.

God called the family to be a place of powerful strength where the man and woman take their rightful place completing one another. In this way, they create an atmosphere in the home for the Spirit of God to have direct access to the children, and God has the ability to work His will inside of every child in that home.

As parents, it's time we shut the door to the devil in our homes by purposing to live in harmony. It's time to rise up. It begins by making Jesus Christ the Lord of your life. I have said to Sharon, "Jesus must be more important to you than I am, Sharon. Jesus is more important to me than you are."

Now, that's hard on a young woman's or a young man's ego when they're caught in an emotional fantasy of who they are and what the relationship is to be. But unless Jesus occupies front and center stage in your life, He has no part in you. Jesus doesn't take a back seat to anyone. Lukewarmness has no place in God's Kingdom; you'll be spewed out of His mouth.

If you have riches, but you don't have Jesus in your life, your riches are corrupted. Every empire you're building will be ashes. Zero. Nothing. If you make All-State or All-American, but don't put Jesus first in your life, it's a zero in God's eyes. If you get your bachelor's or master's or doctorate, but Jesus isn't Lord of your life, that certificate means nothing. You may get a better job, but it means nothing in God's eyes. Only what's done in His will and for His purposes will last.

If there has ever been a time when the Body of Christ should wake up, it's right now. Everything we do must be done in God's purposes and plans.

51

Strengthening the Foundation of Your Family

**If the foundations are destroyed,
What can the righteous do?**

Psalm 11:3

It's time to strengthen the foundation of your family. If you are single, now is the time to build a great foundation in your life should God call you into marriage for the first time or into a remarriage. If your children are grown, God wants to use you to strengthen the marriages of others. It's never too late and you're never too old to have a better marriage.

The word *foundations* in the Hebrew means "basis, moral support, or purpose." If the purpose, the moral support, the foundation, and the basis of your life and your existence are destroyed, what can you do?

As we look historically at America's beginnings, initially the founding fathers of our government — those who met in the congressional convention and those who were part of that first cabinet — were men and women who believed in God, who believed in Jesus Christ as Lord and Savior, and who took the Word of God as the founding principles for the Constitution and for the basic beliefs of our nation. Our government was, for the most part, ruled and directed by the laws of God.

In the early days of our school system, the founding fathers learned to read from the New England primer. They learned their ABCs and grammar by memorizing Scripture. The New England primer was simply Bible verses. Prayer and the Word of God were incorporated into the educational system. Only by going back historically can we see how far we've moved off track from our country's beginnings.

In the early days of our country, society as a whole stood on moral principles and standards based upon God's Word. Prayer was a natural thing. Most of the people who came to America didn't come for gold, but they came because of God. They fled their continent because of religious persecution. The Pilgrims came to America to look for a new and broader relationship with God.

Now, some 200 years later, our government has, by and large, been given over to secular humanism. No longer is the Bible a standard for what's done in the legislative, judicial, or executive branches of government. The standard has become what man thinks is right.

We've taken prayer and the Bible out of our public school systems. Many of today's universities, what we know as state schools, began as schools of ministry. Duke University, with its blue devil mascot, began as a place to train ministers to impact a nation.

As we look at other school systems, a secular humanistic philosophy has taken over the educational process. God is no longer the authority, the Word is no longer the standard by which education is judged, and prayer is no longer incorporated into the educational process.

When we speak of *humanistic,* we're saying that man makes his own decisions and decides what's right and wrong and no longer has a standard called the Word of God to determine what's right and wrong. Man makes himself God in humanism.

When the Bible was removed as a standard, the Supreme Court legalized abortion. A woman can choose, if she decides to, under what is called "necessary circumstances," to take the life of an unborn child. But when you look into the Word of God as a standard, abortion is called "murder." When you throw the Word of God out, humanistic philosophy can do just about anything.

If the foundations of government and the educational system and the mores, rules, and principles of society are destroyed, what can the righteous do?

Today, the remaining two institutions that are under attack and under a barrage of humanistic influence are the family and the Church.

My young boy, John, and I were knocking on doors in a soulwinning outreach. A lady and her two young children about 9 and 13 answered the door. When I told her who I was, she said, "No need talking to me. I'm an atheist."

My little boy had never heard that word.

Then I asked, "If you died today, do you know you would go to heaven?"

"It doesn't make any difference," she answered. "I don't believe there's a God."

She lives just a few blocks from my home. We're living in a society like this today.

Sharon took our son, Paul, with her and was knocking on doors in our soulwinning outreach. She said, "I am amazed at the animosity and attitude toward Christianity of people who live in nice houses and who look very kind."

Many of the people we contacted in our soulwinning outreach talked about being in a church, but they didn't know a thing about being born again. We know in the last days there will be a religious system to which people belong, but they won't be born again.

If we don't arise *now* as individuals and strengthen our families, build the foundations strong, and in some cases rebuild the broken-down foundations, then the pillars of the Church will be undermined. We're under a barrage to let go of the truths of Christianity: to not say that you must be saved by the blood of Jesus Christ, to let go of the gifts of the Spirit, to let go of healing, and to let go of all the fundamental principles of God's Word believed by the original disciples.

Today, entire church associations have pulled out from under the foundation of the Word of God. They no longer believe in healing. They no longer believe in the power of God to deliver. They no longer believe in the virgin birth of Jesus or in the blood of Christ.

It's vital to realize that if we're going to build a pier out in the ocean, that pier is only going to be as strong as the pilings underneath it. When the families in a church start to crumble, the church is affected, so the devil is striking at the families. If you destroy the families, you will crumble the church in its power, influence, impact, and in its ability to save and deliver. It's time to rebuild the foundations.

Many years ago in Europe when the great cathedrals were built, in order to support the arches, the builders used what were called flying buttresses. The support for the high exterior walls was on the outside. That's much like marriages were in America 50 and 75 years ago. Many marriages stayed together, not because of inner strength, but because of outward moral pressure from society. If you got a divorce, you were put down by society. People wouldn't divorce because of public opinion.

Today in America, the outside supports and pressure are not only gone, but they're working to tear down what's on the inside. That means the marriage must have greater inward strength than it has ever had in history.

We're in an hour when you cannot take for granted that you have a strong marriage. You cannot assume that all is well. You must take the attitude, ''I am going to build my marriage and family strong. I am going to continue to strengthen it.'' We must have a fresh new strength hidden within us, like construction that puts strength on the inside, literally hidden from view.

It's time to wake up even if you have a good marriage. You can no longer assume that you can lock it in neutral and not work on it. The storms are coming against every marriage and against every church.

Recently, someone shared with me after the marriage fell apart, ''I put everything and every other person and their needs and situations before my family.''

If the foundations are destroyed, what can the righteous do? If you lose the foundation underneath your marriage, then you've lost your platform for ministering to the world. We need to have the Answer working in us if we're going to export the Answer!

The principles of the Word of God must work in our homes to be an example and a light to others. You must take a stand and decide that your family and your marriage are priority. The long-lasting value of what you will reap in your home will be far greater than the investment you'll make in the worldly systems and the rewards you'll reap from the world.

There's nothing like happiness in the home and children who grow up to serve God and be a blessing in the earth. On the other hand, there's nothing more disastrous and more heartbreaking than for someone to have the world by the tail, to build their own kingdom and amass great wealth, only to see their family fall apart and their children go against God and against them. It tears a person apart.

Jesus said, ''. . . **what will a man give in exchange for his soul?**'' (Matt. 16:26). Let's look at this verse a little differently: ''*What will a man give in exchange for the soul of* *his family?''* God will bless you if you put His Word first in your home and marriage.

Some homes, families, and marriages are like the walls of Jerusalem after Nebuchadnezzar and the Babylonians had destroyed them. The walls are down, and the gates and the strong places that once existed have been burned with fire.

Thank God, the Lord has Nehemiahs who will arise. God sent Nehemiah to the land of captivity, and in a midnight ride, Nehemiah viewed the broken-down walls. He saw the burned gates. He saw the destruction. Nehemiah wept and asked the Lord what he should do. God told him to build the walls up from the ground.

If your walls are down and your gates have been burned, it's time to rebuild.

The Spirit of God spoke through the prophet Joel: **''. . .I will restore to you the years that the swarming locust has eaten, the crawling locust, the consuming locust, and the chewing locust, my great army which I sent among you''** (Joel 2:25).

The Spirit of God spoke through the prophet Isaiah: **''. . .you shall build the old waste places; you shall raise up the foundations of many generations; and you shall be called the Repairer of the Breach, the Restorer of Streets to Dwell In''** (Is. 58:12).

The old waste places are going to be inhabited once again, but we have to determine to rebuild them.

I want to bring you hope, not condemnation. If your walls are down and the gates are burned, you can build again. What the devil has taken can be restored. If the enemy has come in, he can be driven out. If children have been lost, they can be prayed back into the Kingdom of God. If things in your life have been wrecked, God is in the salvage business. It's called ''salvation.''

The word *salvation* comes from the same root word as *salvage*. It means "taking that which is all messed up and ruined and putting it back together again." God is going to do just that in many homes and lives.

It's never too late with God. It's never too late to turn, repent, and reach out to Him.

52

Maturing in Marriage and Family Relationships

The basic cause of the contention in most marriages and families is a lack of maturity. God wants us to be the kind of mature people who can make the marriage and family work.

Mature people are willing to change. Arrogant people don't want to change, but when you humble yourself, then you're willing to make adjustments. Almost any relationship can work if people will make adjustments.

Change comes from desire, and when you desire for your marriage and family to be better, you'll work to make it happen.

Immature people can't find happiness in a marriage because of their own selfishness. People bump from one marriage or relationship to another because of immaturity. It's time to start building the inward supports of a mature life that humbles itself and says, "God, I need Your help."

Someone said to me, "It seems that two parents with beautiful children would make any sacrifice possible to save their children." We live in a society today that's willing to sacrifice their beautiful children on the altar of the divorce court to satisfy their own egos. They say, "Forget the children. The concern is my feelings and what's happening to me."

A mature person is willing to say, "I was wrong; please forgive me." An immature person, however, will say, *"If I was wrong,* I apologize." That never goes over big!

A mature person will say, "What can I do to make things better?"

A mature person will say, "How can I help you?" That's servanthood being put into practice: "How can things go better for you?" Some people are afraid to ask because they're afraid they'll get an answer! But God hasn't given you that spirit of fear. It's okay to ask.

A mature person will say, "Here's where I need help."

A mature person will resolve differences without anger and without throwing pots and pans! Maturity can sit down, talk, and discuss.

53

When Are You Mature Enough for Marriage?

You are mature enough for marriage *when you understand God's plans and purposes for marriage.* Many people aren't mature enough, because they've never understood God's plans and purposes.

You're mature enough for marriage *when you're willing to assume the responsibilities of being a husband, a wife, a father, or a mother.*

You're mature enough to get married *when you're ready to settle down with one person for the rest of your life.* You should think in terms of a 75-year contract. When you're ready to sign in blood with your life, you're ready for marriage.

You're ready for marriage *when you're no longer depending upon your family or relatives to support you.* Thank God for support that may come, but you shouldn't depend on it when you're going into a marriage union. You need to fly with your own wings. Many people want to get married, but they set themselves up for difficulties by their financial circumstances.

You are ready to get married *when you are ready to give love and to be loved.* Many couples get married in lust and the husband and wife have never learned to really love one another. When they say, "I don't love you anymore," what they're really saying is, "I don't lust after you anymore." The lust is gone, so there's no reason to stay in the relationship. But when that love is self-giving, kind, and tenderhearted, then you're ready for marriage, because regardless of circumstances, you'll keep on loving.

If you're married and you've missed some of these foundational stones, you must work at it. You must desire to the point that your desire is translated into effort to rebuild the foundations in your marriage. Some people want a better marriage, but they don't translate the desire into effort.

God dealt with me that both Sharon and I were to read Larry Christensen's book, *The Christian Family,*[1] before we got married. It strengthened the foundation for our marriage. This book has been written to help you.

You need to take time to talk about ways to improve and strengthen your home. Learn to ask: ''How can I help you? What can I do?'' Open yourself up to listen, talk, and communicate. You can have a seminar just between the husband and wife! I don't think it's always the issue of getting new information. I think people have enough information in many cases if they'll communicate it with each other.

In some cases, the added input of a Christian marriage counselor, someone who has dealt with marriages and families, can add strength to your marriage.

To be mature enough for marriage, *you need to be healed of past hurts.* You cannot carry grudges into a marriage and family relationship and expect the family to keep growing. If you're bitter at your children, the children are bitter at the parents, or the husband and wife are bitter at each other, you need to forgive and release one another. If you don't, when an argument or strife comes and your blood pressure goes up, you'll pull out your list and go through all the things that have happened in the last 20 years or so!

---

[1](Minneapolis: Bethany Fellowship, Inc., 1970).

You need to have a list-burning ceremony! Send the offenses up in smoke! Burn them and determine, *"I am going to forgive myself, forgive my mate, and forgive my children."*

54

A New Beginning

When two born-again believers come together in marriage before God, in His eyes, they stand cleansed. They're as clean before the Lord as Adam and Eve were in the Garden before they sinned, no matter what their past has been.

Maybe you've had a broken marriage and you've remarried. There's cleansing and forgiveness for failures that have been committed in the past, whether you've deliberately or unknowingly failed in marriage. God can give you knowledge and understanding. He can give you a marriage in wholeness and bring into your marriage the power that He plans.

You can start over today right where you are with a fresh mental and spiritual attitude, by forgetting those things which are behind.

You can start by obeying 2 Chronicles 7:14:

"If My people who are called by My name will humble themselves, and pray and seek My face, and turn from their wicked ways, then I will hear from heaven, and will forgive their sin and heal their land."

This means, for a fresh start and for a healing in your marriage and family, you need to:

1. *Humble yourself.*

2. *Pray and seek God's face.*

3. *Turn from your wicked ways.*

Then God will hear you, He'll forgive your sin, and He'll heal your marriage and family.

To assure a new beginning, obey the command of Isaiah 60:1 (AMP):

> **Arise [from the depression and prostration in which circumstances have kept you; rise to a new life]! Shine — be radiant with the glory of the Lord; for your light is come, and the glory of the Lord is risen upon you!**

Arise from the circumstances in which you find yourself. You can rise above them, and God will meet your every need. *He wants your marriage healed.* It's not too late for your marriage. It's never too late. God's Word is the same yesterday, today, and forever. (Heb. 13:8.)

55

Framing Your Marriage and Family With God's Blessings

I have translated Deuteronomy 28:1-14 into a prayer of confession with which you can *daily* frame your marriage and family. Believe and receive these blessings today, and as a result, your relationships will be enriched as never before.

"Because we diligently obey the voice of the Lord our God and all of His commandments, He will set my marriage and family on high above all nations of the earth.

"All of His blessings will come upon us and overtake us, because we obey His voice.

"Blessed shall we be in the city, and blessed shall we be in the country.

"Blessed shall be the fruit of our body, the produce of our ground and the increase of our herds, the increase of our cattle and the offspring of our flocks.

"Blessed shall be our basket and kneading bowl.

"Blessed shall we be when we come in, and blessed shall we be when we go out.

"The Lord will cause our enemies who rise against us to be defeated before our face; they shall come against us one way and flee before us seven ways.

"The Lord will command the blessing on us in our storehouses and in all to which we set our hands, and He will bless us in the land which the Lord our God is giving us.

"*The Lord will establish us as a holy people to Himself, just as He has sworn to us, if we keep His commandments and walk in His ways.*

"*Then all peoples of the earth shall see that we are called by the name of the Lord, and they shall be afraid of us.*

"*And the Lord will grant us plenty of goods, in the fruit of our body, in the increase of our livestock, and in the produce of our ground, in the land to which the Lord swore to our fathers to give us.*

"*The Lord will open to us His good treasure, the heavens to give the rain to our land in its season and to bless all the work of our hands. We shall lend to many, but we shall not borrow.*

"*And the Lord will make us the head and not the tail; we shall be above only, and not beneath, if we heed the commandments of the Lord God, which He commands us today and we are careful to observe them.*

"*We shall not turn aside from any of the words which God commands us this day, to the right hand or to the left, to go after other gods to serve them.*"

Receive these blessings in your personal life, in your marriage, in your family, and in your home, in Jesus' name. Amen.

References

The *King James Version* (KJV) of the Bible.

The Amplified Bible (AMP), *Old Testament* copyright © 1965, 1987 by The Zondervan Corporation. *New Testament* copyright © 1958, 1987 by the Lockman Foundation. Used by permission.

The *New Testament in Modern English*, (Rev. Ed.) by J.B. Phillips. Copyright © 1958, 1960, 1972 by J.B. Phillips. Reprinted by permission of Macmillian Publishing Co., New York, New York.

The Holy Bible: New International Version (NIV). Copyright © 1973, 1978, 1984 by the International Bible Society. Used by permission of Zondervan Bible Publishers.

Billy Joe Daugherty, Pastor of Victory Christian Center in Tulsa, Oklahoma, is a soulwinner with a world vision.

He is founder of Victory Christian School, Victory Bible Institute and Victory World Mission Training Center with the goals of training students to be effective Christians worldwide.

Believing that "the greatest tool of evangelism in the coming days will be the local church," Billy Joe emphasizes the ministry of the individual believer in the many outreaches of Victory Christian Center.

Graduates of Oral Roberts University, he and his wife, Sharon, have traveled extensively around the country ministering the Word of God and the love of God.

Billy Joe's daily radio and television programs are bringing encouragement and sound teaching into many homes.

To contact
the author,
write:

Billy Joe Daugherty
Victory Christian Center
7700 S. Lewis
Tulsa, Oklahoma 74136-7700

*Please include your prayer requests
and comments when you write.*

Other Books by Billy Joe Daugherty

This New Life
Absolute Victory
Faith Power
Death Is Not the End
Be on Fire for the Lord
The Fear of the Lord
Diligence Produces Results
Exceedingly Abundantly
You Are Valuable
Overcoming the Storms of Life
You Can Be Healed

Books by Sharon Daugherty

A Fruitful Life, Walking in the Spirit
Called By His Side

**Available from your local bookstore,
or by writing:**

Victory Christian Center
7700 South Lewis • Tulsa, OK 74136
(or calling: 918-493-1700)

or

Harrison House
P.O. Box 35035 • Tulsa, OK 74153

The Harrison House Vision

Proclaiming the truth and the power
Of the Gospel of Jesus Christ
With excellence;

Challenging Christians to
Live victoriously,
Grow spiritually,
Know God Intimately.